PRAISE FOR THE
UNCOMMON JUNIOR HIGH GROUP STUDIES

The *Uncommon* Junior High curriculum will help God's Word to become real for your students.
Larry Acosta
Founder of the Hispanic Ministry Center, Urban Youth Workers Institute

The best junior high/middle school curriculum to come out in years.
Jim Burns, Ph.D.
President of HomeWord (www.homeword.com)

A rich resource that makes genuine connections with middle school students and the culture in which they live.
Mark W. Cannister
Professor of Christian Ministries, Gordon College, Wenham, Massachusetts

A landmark resource for years to come.
Chapman R. Clark, Ph.D.
Professor of Youth, Family and Culture, Fuller Theological Seminary

Great biblical material, creative interaction and *user friendly*! What more could you ask for? I highly recommend it!
Ken Davis
Author and Speaker (www.kendavis.com)

A fresh tool . . . geared to make a lasting impact.
Paul Fleischmann
President and Co-founder of the National Network of Youth Ministries

The *Uncommon* Junior High curriculum capitalizes both GOD and TRUTH.
Monty L. Hipp
President, The C4 Group (www.c4group.nonprofitsites.com)

The *Uncommon* Junior High curriculum is truly cross-cultural.
Walt Mueller
Founder and President, Center for Parent/Youth Understanding (www.cpyu.org)

The creators and writers of this curriculum know and love young teens, and that's what sets good junior high curriculum apart from the mediocre stuff!

Mark Oestreicher
Author, Speaker and Consultant (www.markoestreicher.com)

This is serious curriculum for junior-highers! Not only does it take the great themes of the Christian faith seriously, but it takes junior-highers seriously as well.

Wayne Rice
Founder and Director, Understanding Your Teenager (www.waynerice.com)

The *Uncommon* Junior High curriculum fleshes out two absolute essentials for great curriculum: biblical depth and active learning.

Duffy Robbins
Professor of Youth Ministry, Eastern University, St. Davids, Pennsylvania

It's about time that curriculum took junior-highers and youth workers seriously.

Rich Van Pelt
President of Alongside Consulting, Denver, Colorado

The *Uncommon* Junior High curriculum will help leaders bring excellence to every lesson while enjoying the benefit of a simplified preparation time.

Lynn Ziegenfuss
Mentoring Project Director, National Network of Youth Ministries

THE NEW TESTAMENT

KARA POWELL
General Editor

Published by Gospel Light
Ventura, California, U.S.A.
www.gospellight.com
Printed in the U.S.A.

Unit 1, "The Kingdom of God Is Near," adapted from Pulse #5: *Followers of Jesus.*
Unit 2, "The Kingdom of God Is Growing," adapted from Pulse #14: *Reaching Your World.*

Contributing writers: Kara Powell, PhD; Donna Fitzpatrick; Christi Goeser;
Jeff Mattesich; Laurie Polich; Siv Ricketts; John and Betsy Wilson.

Library of Congress Cataloging-in-Publication Data
Uncommon jr. high group study : the New Testament / Kara Powell, general editor ;
[contributing writers, Donna Fitzpatrick . . . et al.].
p. cm.
Includes bibliographical references.
ISBN 978-0-8307-5522-6 (trade paper)
1. Bible. N.T.—Study and teaching. 2. Christian education of teenagers. I. Powell, Kara. II.
Fitzpatrick, Donna. III. Title: Uncommon junior high group study.
BS2530.U52 2010
225.071'2—dc22
2010011511

Rights for publishing this book outside the U.S.A. or in non-English languages are
administered by Gospel Light Worldwide, an international not-for-profit ministry.
For additional information, please visit www.glww.org, email info@glww.org, or write
to Gospel Light Worldwide, 1957 Eastman Avenue, Ventura, CA 93003, U.S.A.

To order copies of this book and other Gospel Light products in bulk quantities,
please contact us at 1-800-446-7735.

Contents

How to Use the *Uncommon* Junior High Group Studies 7

UNIT I: THE KINGDOM OF GOD IS NEAR

Session 1: Mary and Martha: Wholehearted Devotion 11
Session 2: The Generous Widow: Wholehearted Giving 29
Session 3: Zack Attack: Wholehearted Surrender 45
Session 4: The Centurion: A Trusting Faith 61
Session 5: The Four Friends: An Active Faith 75
Session 6: The Leper: A Desperate Faith 93
Conclusion: Get to Know the Four Gospels 109

UNIT II: THE KINGDOM OF GOD IS GROWING

Session 7: Empowered by the Holy Spirit 113
Session 8: From Denier to Defender 127
Session 9: Let's Eat 139
Session 10: From Killer to Crusader 151
Session 11: Out of the Frying Pan and into the Fire 165
Session 12: A Link in the Chain 177
Conclusion: The Acts Challenge 189

Endnotes 191

How to Use the *Uncommon* Junior High Group Studies

Each *Uncommon* junior high group study contains 12 sessions, which are divided into 2 stand-alone units of 6 sessions each. You may choose to teach all 12 sessions consecutively, or to use just one unit, or to present each session separately. You know your group, so do what works best for you and your students.

This is your leader's guidebook for teaching your group. Electronic files (in PDF format) for each session's student handouts are available online at **www.gospellight.com/uncommon/jh_the_new_testament.zip**. The handouts include the "Reflect" section of each study, formatted for easy printing, in addition to any student worksheets for the session. You may print as many copies as you need for your group.

Each individual session begins with a brief overview of the "big idea" of the lesson, the aims of the session, the primary Bible verse and additional verses that tie in to the topic being discussed. Each of the 12 sessions is geared to be 45 to 90 minutes in length and is comprised of two options that you can choose from, based on the type of group that you have. Option 1 tends to be a more active learning experience, while Option 2 tends to be a more discussion-oriented exercise.

The sections in each session are as follows:

Starter
Young people will stay in your youth group longer if they feel comfortable and make friends. This first section helps students get to know each other better and focus on the theme of the lesson in a fun and engaging way.

Message
The Message section enables students to look up to God by relating the words of Scripture to the session topic.

Dig

Unfortunately, many young people are biblically illiterate. In this section, students look inward and discover how God's Word connects with their own world.

Apply

Young people need the opportunity to think through the issues at hand. The apply section leads students out into their world with specific challenges to apply at school, at home and with their friends.

Reflect

This concluding section of the study allows students to reflect on the material presented in the session. You can print these pages from the PDF found at **www.gospellight.com/uncommon/jh_the_new_testament.zip** and give them to your students as a handout for them to work on throughout the week.

Want More Options?

An additional option for each section, along with accompanying worksheets, is available in PDF format at **www.gospellight.com/uncommon/jh_the_new_testament.zip**.

UNIT I

The Kingdom of God
Is Near

Recently at a Christian music festival I was struck by the superstar status showered on the musicians as fans swarmed to catch a glimpse of their favorite Christian band. A few minutes later, my focus turned to another band of Christians ministering at the festival without any audience at all. Largely invisible, these individuals roamed the grounds picking up trash, setting out food, counseling troubled kids or praying silently in a corner. And though no one appeared to notice them, I couldn't help but wonder from God's view where the real stage was—in the limelight or in the quiet acts of service. Or maybe in both.

Often when we teach Scripture, we make it a point to tell stories of Peter. But what about Andrew? If it weren't for Andrew's faithfulness and concern for his brother that led him to introduce Peter to Jesus, we would never have heard about Peter. Similarly, Levi was not one of the more celebrated disciples, yet his calling helped people see that even a sinner could become a follower of Jesus. His conversion also produced one of the four Gospels, for Levi was also known as Matthew.

And what about those whose names we'll never know? An unnamed centurion in Matthew 8 takes Jesus at His word and is held up as a prime example of faith. A widow in Mark 12 demonstrates what giving really means. And in Mark 2, four friends go to a great deal of trouble to carry a friend to Jesus for healing.

This unit uses these stories to offer hope to your junior-highers—some of whom feel nameless and lost in the crowd—and to introduce the four canonical Gospels. As your students work their way through this study, they will see the importance of each person's story—including their own. If you want the stories in this book to have full impact on your students, try some of the following:

- **Practice telling good stories**. Have you ever heard someone say that we have to "make the stories of the Bible come alive"? In a sense, that's not really true . . . the stories of the Bible *are* alive! But sometimes the details we give, the way that we help students understand what each character was thinking and feeling, and the way we help students feel as if they were actually there—even if that might mean wearing a tunic or carrying a prop—will help the life of the stories shine clearly.

- **Tell your own story.** Students love hearing about *you*, especially what you went through when you were their age. Take a few minutes to dig deep in your memory to remember what you felt like when you walked onto your junior high campus, how you related to your parents and what you wanted from your friends. Be courageous and share your junior high pictures with them. When the giggling stops, your students will be more open to what you have to say because they'll know you can understand them.

- **Ask others to share their stories.** Who are the adults that students respect in your church or community? Invite them to come in and share how they felt in junior high, especially when it connects with the "big idea" of that week's lesson. From senior pastors to parents to local TV celebrities, students love getting the inside scoop on their heroes.

The more students are connected to these stories, the more they will be inspired to live out their own stories with faith, courage, joy and excitement. In the end, we'll all realize that our true audience is really only an audience of One: Jesus Christ.

Laurie Polich
Pastor of Small Groups and Discipleship
Ocean Hills Covenant Church
Santa Barbara, California

MARY AND MARTHA: WHOLEHEARTED DEVOTION

THE BIG IDEA

The everyday details of life can distract us from giving our undivided attention to God.

SESSION AIMS

In this session, you will guide students to (1) learn that Jesus places time with Him ahead of everything else; (2) understand the effects of spending time with Jesus; and (3) act by committing to spend time with Jesus this week.

THE BIGGEST VERSE

"Mary has chosen what is better, and it will not be taken away from her" (Luke 10:42).

OTHER IMPORTANT VERSES

Matthew 5:14-16; Luke 10:7-8,38-42; John 15:5; Romans 12:13; 1 Peter 4:9

Note: Additional options and worksheets in $8^1/_2$" x 11" format for this session are available for download at **www.gospellight.com/uncommon/jh_the_new_testament.zip**.

STARTER

Option 1: Water Balloon Hot Potato. For this option, you need a five-minute timer and four or five balloons filled with water. (*Note:* It might be best if this activity were done outside! If that's not possible, lay down a large plastic tarp where the activity will take place.)

Greet students and ask for five volunteers to come up front and sit in a circle (in chairs or on the floor). Let them know that they are going to play a type of Hot Potato game with water balloons, so volunteers should be willing to get wet. Explain that you will ask the first contestant a question and he or she can only pass the water balloon when he or she answers the question. Once the question is answered, the water balloon is passed to the next contestant, who must give a new and different answer to the same question before he or she can pass the water balloon to the next person (no repeating answers). Whoever has the water balloon when the timer goes off is out and gets doused with the contents of the balloon!

Some question ideas include the following:

- What is an excuse teenagers give for not doing their homework?
- What things do people do to waste time?
- What things do you do with your friends?
- What is a dreaded chore around the house?

Set the timer for one minute (or for more unpredictable fun, set the timer at random *short* amounts of time) and begin the game. After you've eliminated all but one of the volunteers, stop the game and invite the volunteers to return to their seats. (*Option:* If time allows, ask for five new volunteers, but don't drag the game out too long or nonparticipating students will lose interest.)

Ask the group to identify things that can distract teens from spending time with God. Answers might include TV, video games, sports, music rehearsals, dance classes, movies, friends, homework, magazines, books, chores, sleep, and so forth.

Discuss why these things often come before God. (Answers might include because they're fun to do, they're distracting, they have deadlines, they're easier to do, and so on.) Then suggest that sometimes it's simply because spending time with God doesn't even come to mind.

Ask the group members if they ever feel that life just gets too busy to spend time with God because they simply have too much going on, or they're stressed out because of school, or they have too many extra activities, or their parents seem impossible to please. Explain that we've all felt that way at some point in our lives. Today, you're going to look at how two lesser-known followers of Christ learned about the value of time and the best way to spend it.

Option 2: Timetable. For this option, you need a video recorder and screen to present the video, a few volunteers for voice-overs, copies of "Timetable" (found on the next page) and pens or pencils. (*Optional:* Get extra "actors" for the school scene.) Ahead of time, create a brief video as if the camera is you and the audience is looking through your eyes. The scenario should be something like this:

> You (the camera) wake up to a buzzing alarm clock. You yawn and rub your eyes (the camera lens) while you mumble to yourself that you need to do your devotions. Just as you open your Bible to read, your mom calls out for you to feed the dog and eat your breakfast. Put the Bible down and stop filming.
>
> Open a new scene by picking up your Bible again. Just as you begin to read this time, your dad yells at you for leaving the video game stuff out all over the living room and tells you to come clean it up. After doing that, you only have enough time to jump into the shower and run off to school. (You can show this part by filming your hands turning on the shower.) The next scene shows your Bible lying on your bed where you left it and the audience hears you telling your mom that you're leaving for school.

If you decide to tape some at-school scenes, take some volunteers to visit a local junior high campus (or "fake" it at a similar location, such as a park) and film them acting as students during a snack break, talking about how hard the history or math test was. The final shots should be after school: watching TV, doing homework, calling friends, practicing sports, playing video games, eating

Youth Leader Tip
Junior-highers get bored easily, especially with homemade videos, so make sure your clips are short and fast-paced. Add upbeat music in the background to keep your students engaged and awake!

Things I Do	Time I Spend Doing Them

dinner—anything that will take you to bedtime, when you notice your Bible still lying where you left it on your bed that morning and you suddenly realize that you didn't spend any time with God today. As you are drifting off to sleep, you promise yourself, "Tomorrow I won't get distracted and I'll spend time with God" and the video ends.

Greet students and let them know that they're going to watch a short video. After the video, distribute "Timetable" and pens or pencils. Ask students to make a list of the things that distract them from spending time with God. Next to each item, ask them to list the number of hours they spend per week on that activity; then circle the top five activities that use the most time.

Ask a few students to each share an item, and after each item is shared, ask the rest of the class to vote whether that is typically a good or bad use of time. Vote on a few items, and then ask the following:

- Are most of the things that we listed on the worksheets bad? (*No.*)
- When can something that is neutral—or even good—become bad? (*When it takes priority over relationships with other people and our time with God.*)

Continue by asking the group if they ever feel like their lives just get too busy to spend time with God—that they simply have too much going on in their lives. Do they ever feel stressed out because of school and all their extra activities? (You'll probably hear a resounding "yes!") Conclude by stating that today, you're going to look at how two lesser-known followers of Christ learned about the value of time and how to best use it.

MESSAGE

Option 1: Judge Rudy. For this option, you need several Bibles, eight copies of "Judge Rudy and the Case of Martha v. Mary" (found on the next page), two tables (one each for the plaintiff and the defendant), a podium or table for the judge, whatever props you can easily obtain (such as a gavel, a wig and a big black dress or robe for Judge Rudy), and a large character name card for each of the following cast members to hang around his or her neck: "Judge Rudy," "Jury" (three of these), "Bailiff," "Mary," "Martha" and "Jesus." (*Note:* this skit can also be prepared in advance with adult staff and/or students or performed spontaneously by giving each participant a script to read from as the skit is performed. Either way, *you* should act the part of Judge Rudy.)

Judge Rudy and the Case of Martha v. Mary

The Cast: Judge Rudy; Bailiff; Martha; Mary; three jurors
The Props: Black robe or dress; white wig; gavel; podium or table (for judge); seven chairs; two tables (plaintiff and defendant); seven character nametags made from posterboard with a string attached to hang around the characters' necks; a large Bible

The courtroom scene is set with two tables, one for the plaintiff and one for the defendant, and a podium (or another table) for the judge. Jurors are sitting in a row at the side. Each character is wearing a large name card around his or her neck. Everyone except the judge (who is offstage) is sitting down. Judge Rudy is wearing a wig and a big black robe or dress and carrying a gavel.

Bailiff: (*Stands up.*) All rise for the Honorable Judge Rudy.
Judge: (*Enters and takes the bench.*) Be seated. Let's see. What have we got on the docket today?
Bailiff: Martha v. Mary, your Honor.
Judge: What's the complaint?
Bailiff: Martha is suing for damages due to her sister's laziness and lack of help at a dinner party they hosted.
Judge: Martha, you may take the stand.
Bailiff: (*Holding large Bible.*) Raise your right hand and place your left hand on the Bible. Do you swear to tell the truth, the whole truth and nothing but the truth, so help you God?
Martha: (*Raising her hand*) I do.
Judge: You may begin.
Martha: Well, Your Honor, the other night my sister and I decided to have a friend over for dinner. When He arrived, there were still plenty of things that needed to be finished. The salad wasn't made, I had a roast in the oven that needed to be basted every five minutes, the table wasn't set, and drinks needed to be served. But instead of helping me take care of all these things, she (*pointing at Mary*) went and sat with our guest and completely ignored my pleas for help. I finally couldn't take it anymore and practically had a nervous breakdown. I am still suffering with headaches every time I think about it (*whining as she takes hold of her aching head*).
Judge: Thank you, Martha, you may be seated. (*Martha returns to the plaintiff's table.*) Those are serious charges. Mary, please take the stand. (*Waits for Mary to take the witness stand.*)
Bailiff: (*Holding large Bible.*) Raise your right hand and place your left hand on the Bible. Do you swear to tell the truth, the whole truth and nothing but the truth, so help you God?
Mary: I do.
Judge: How do you plead?
Mary: Well, Your Honor, I suppose I'm (*pause*) . . . guilty.
Jury: (*Looking shocked, gasping and talking amongst themselves*) Oh my . . . what did she say? . . . can you believe it?
Judge: You are pleading guilty to these charges?
Mary: Well, yes . . . but I do have an explanation.
Judge: This had better be a good one!
Mary: Your Honor, our guest wasn't just any old guest; it was Jesus. The way I look at it is: How can you spend too much time with the Son of God? Isn't He really more important than whether we had salad or if the roast has been basted every five minutes? He is my Savior and my Lord, and He is my priority. Everything else is second to Him. My sister must understand that Jesus deserves our attention even if we think we are too busy.
Judge: Jesus was your dinner guest, huh? That guy sure gets a lot of free meals. (*Clears throat.*) Anyway, under the circumstances, I see why you did not worry about the details that concerned your sister. Case dismissed! (*Hits gavel.*)
Mary: Thank you, Your Honor.

Ahead of time, set up the courtroom: Place the judge's podium in front of the audience behind the plaintiff's and defendant's tables, the jury chairs off to one side and a chair for the witness next to the judge on the same side as the jury, facing the audience. Ask for seven volunteers to act out a skit. Distribute "Judge Rudy and the Case of Martha v. Mary" to each volunteer and assign characters by giving volunteers each a character name card. Instruct the enthusiastic actors to take their positions in the "courtroom" (Jesus is to sit with the audience) and begin the skit.

When the skit is finished and the spontaneous standing ovation subsides, distribute the Bibles and explain that courtroom observers typically don't find out the actual truth of what happened because the plaintiff and defendant each has his or her version of the story, and only certain information is allowable in the courtroom. Fortunately, we *do* have the facts about this particular situation today.

Explain that four different followers of Jesus wrote accounts of His life, ministry, death and resurrection. We call these accounts "the Gospels," and they are the New Testament books of Matthew, Mark, Luke and John. We often study one story at a time from these books, as we will do today, but it's important to remember that the stories we highlight from Jesus' life are small parts of His bigger story: the story of God's project to save the world.

Choose two volunteers to read every other verse from Luke 10:38-42, and then discuss the following:

- How are we similar to Martha? (*We often make less important things a priority over spending time with God.*)

- Was Martha doing a bad thing by focusing on preparing the meal and wanting Mary's help? Why or why not? (*She wasn't necessarily doing a bad thing, but her priorities were misplaced. We often think that other things need to get done before we can spend time with God.*)

- Why do you think Martha didn't understand Mary's choice? (*She lost perspective and became overwhelmed with details, losing track of what was truly important—spending time with Jesus. She might have felt a need to have everything perfect for Jesus and the other guests.*)

- What makes Mary's choice better? (*Because she chose to spend time with Jesus. All the other things that distract us or take our time will mean*

*nothing in heaven. Getting to know Jesus better, on the other hand, will
mean everything.)*[1]

- So does that mean Martha should not have worried about feeding her
  family and her guests? (*Jesus views domestic hospitality positively [see
  Luke 10:7-8] and Paul encouraged it [see Romans 12:13; 1 Peter 4:9], so
  a better solution might have been to spend time with Him first and then
  prepare a simple meal without fussing about unimportant details or trying
  to impress someone.*)

- Why does it seem so hard to fit Jesus into our daily lives? (*We lose track
  of what's most important. If we step back and look at our lives in perspective, we will see and understand why Jesus must come first and that everything else is secondary.*)

- Jesus said only one thing is needed: Him. Do you think that's true? Why
  or why not? (*He is everything we need. In John 15:5, Jesus said, "I am the
  vine; you are the branches. If a man remains in me and I in him, he will
  bear much fruit; apart from me you can do nothing."*)

Transition to the next option by inviting students to ask themselves, *Am I
making excuses like Martha did, explaining away my lack of attention to Jesus, or
am I giving Jesus the attention and priority He deserves in my life?*

Option 2: D-E-F-E-N-S-E. For this option, you will need several Bibles, copies of
"D-E-F-E-N-S-E" (found on the next page), and pens or pencils. Divide students
into groups of three or four and distribute "D-E-F-E-N-S-E" and pens or pencils
to each group. Explain that four different followers of Jesus wrote accounts of
His life, ministry, death and resurrection. We call these accounts "the Gospels,"
and they are the New Testament books of Matthew, Mark, Luke and John. We
often study one story at a time from these books, as we will do today, but it's
important to remember that the stories we highlight from Jesus' life are small
parts of His bigger story: the story of God's project to save the world.

Ask each group to read Luke 10:38-42 and develop a defense for Martha
by outlining excuses Martha might have had for her actions. When a group finishes Martha's defense, it can move on to complete part two of the handout,
with students discussing and writing down reasons why they often don't make
Jesus a priority in their own lives.

D-E-F-E-N-S-E

Reasons Martha didn't spend time with Jesus (see Luke 10:38-42)	Reasons we don't spend time with Jesus

Allow six to eight minutes of discussion, and then invite the groups to share their insights and discuss the following questions:

- How are we similar to Martha? (*We often make less important things a priority over spending time with God.*)

- Was Martha doing a bad thing in focusing on preparing the meal and wanting Mary's help? Why or why not? (*No, it is easy to understand that she would feel that way. We often think that other things need to get done before we can spend time with God.*)

- Why do you think Martha didn't understand Mary's choice? (*She lost perspective and became overwhelmed with details, losing track of what was truly important—spending time with Jesus.*)

- What makes Mary's choice better? (*She chose to spend time with Jesus. All the other things that distract us or take our time will mean nothing in heaven. Getting to know Jesus, on the other hand, will mean everything.*)

- So does that mean Martha should not have worried about feeding her family and her guests? (*Jesus views domestic hospitality positively [see Luke 10:7-8] and Paul encouraged it [see Romans 12:13; 1 Peter 4:9], so a better solution would have been to spend time with Him first and then prepare a simple meal without fussing about unimportant details or trying to impress someone.*)

- Why does it seem so hard to fit Jesus into our own lives? (*We lose track of what's most important. If we step back and look at our lives in perspective, we will see and understand why Jesus must come first and that everything else is secondary.*)

- Do you think what Jesus said was true: only one thing is needed? Why or why not? (*He is everything we need. In John 15:5, Jesus said, "I am the vine; you are the branches. If a man remains in me and I in him, he will bear much fruit; apart from me you can do nothing."*)

Transition to the next option by inviting students to ask themselves, *Am I making excuses like Martha did, explaining away my lack of attention to Jesus, or am I giving Jesus the attention and priority He deserves in my life?*

DIG

Option 1: A Question of Priorities. For this option, you need a willingness to wrestle with students to find the truth. Discuss the following questions:

- If Jesus knows everything about me already, why should I talk with Him? *(Have you ever gone to an amusement park and ridden on all the roller coasters and then enjoyed recalling with your friends the fun you had long after that day was over? Jesus is there for you, waiting to listen as you recall your day—both the high and low points.)*

- How do I explain how Jesus affects me to someone who doesn't believe in God? *(Let people see that Jesus affects you. If you claim to be a Christian, but there isn't any difference between you and your non-Christian friends, then they probably aren't going to see Jesus affecting you. If, however, you are spending time with God and praying that He will give you strength to do what is right, people are going to see a difference. It is equally important that you are real about your struggles, by admitting that it's hard for you not to cheat, gossip or tease. When you do mess up—and we all do—apologize and explain that it is your true desire to not act that way. We are to seek God's strength and the Holy Spirit's power to do what is right and to hold on to His grace when we blow it.)*

- If spending time with God is so good for me, why doesn't He make it easier? *(God has given us free will to choose what we do. If He made it easy for us, we wouldn't be choosing to spend time with Him. Just as we appreciate it when people we care about make a special effort to spend time with us, God wants us to consciously choose to spend time with Him.)*

- Does that mean I should spend all my time with God and never do anything else? *(God is always with you, wherever you are. Since you can talk to Him at any time, you can spend time with Him in science class, while*

Youth Leader Tip

It is important for students to share their ideas. It is equally important to watch your reactions to off-the-wall answers. A simple nod or "okay" can allow you to pass by these moments and stay focused.

you're riding your bike or while you're snacking after school. After all, He
wants us to spend time with other people and develop the gifts and talents
He has given us, but He also wants us to acknowledge that He is with us
all the time and that we can talk with Him whenever we want.)

Option 2: Skating for Jesus. For this option, you need several Bibles, a whiteboard and a dry-erase marker. Begin by reading the following story:

Jason woke up really early one morning—as a matter of fact, he had had
a hard time sleeping the night before. Maybe it was the fact that he was
at camp in a not-so-comfy bunk or maybe it was that he couldn't stop
thinking about what the speaker had asked the campers: "Does your
life really count? Or is it meaningless and empty?"

Jason had to think about that one. As he looked at his life, he saw
a lot of cool stuff. He was captain of the football team and was dating
the most popular eighth-grade girl, even though he was only in seventh
grade. He was a part of his church youth group and went on all the
trips. He did pretty well in school and most of the teachers liked him.

The two things he enjoyed the most, though, were skateboarding
and playing the drums. If there was ever any free time after those two
activities, it usually went to TV or video games. He thought life was
good; at least he was having fun. *What did that guy mean, "Does my life*
count?" I've always thought it counted, but what if I'm wrong?

Jason spent the whole day pondering the question and began to
wonder whether all the things in his life really satisfied him. Finally, he
decided to go talk to the speaker. As they talked, the speaker asked Jason if he had a relationship with Jesus. Jason answered, "Oh yes, I've
basically grown up in the church."

The speaker said, "That's not what I mean. Do you know Jesus
yourself? Do you spend any time with Him? Do you literally have a relationship with Him like you do with a friend?"

Jason hesitated and then replied, "Well, I'm not sure. I thought I
did, but it's more that I go to church and stuff."

"You see, Jason," said the speaker, "all of those things you do are
fine. But if you don't have a relationship with Jesus and put Him *first* in
your life, all those other things are simply time fillers until you die. If you
make Jesus your first priority, not only will you find a purpose, but He
will have an impact on everything that you do."

"What do you mean?" asked Jason.

"Well, you said you like skateboarding, right?"

"Yeah."

"Imagine if you spent every morning with Jesus for 10 or 15 minutes, learning about Him and praying; He would begin to affect you. Next thing you know you aren't just skateboarding for fun, but you have a purpose."

"Really? What is it?" Jason asked.

"That's what you have to find out. It might be that God wants you to reach out to the other skaters who don't know Jesus. Or it might be that He wants to use you as an example for other students. Maybe it's just that He wants you to skate for Him instead of yourself. Whatever it is, it has an eternal purpose, not just filling time."

Now discuss the following questions with the group:

- If you are a skater who makes Jesus your first priority, how might that impact your skateboarding or the people you skate with?
- If you have a big homework assignment and you make Jesus your first priority, how might that affect your homework and your grades?
- If you're an athlete and Jesus is number one in your life, how will your relationship with Him affect the way you prepare, play and interact with other players?

Divide students into groups of three or four and instruct them to pick one activity per group to discuss how making Jesus number one might impact that activity. Allow three or four minutes, and then ask the groups to share their responses, highlighting their answers on the whiteboard.

APPLY

Option 1: Ripple Effect. You will need a copy of "Prayer Journal" (found on the next page) for each student, pens or pencils, a sample entry from a real prayer journal, a bowl filled with water and a pebble or marble. Instruct students to gather around and watch as you drop the pebble into the middle of the bowl filled with water. Point out the ripple that moves from the middle to the outside of the bowl, and then explain that you are going to create the same effect using a volunteer as a pebble and the rest of the group as the water.

Prayer Journal

Date Asked	Prayer Request	Answer	Date Answered

Position students in a circle and ask for a volunteer to stand in the middle. The volunteer leans toward one side of the circle, and the students on that side use their arms to start a ripple like the wave at a sports game with the ripple continuing around the circle. Have students do this a couple of times, and then ask the "pebble" what it is like to see the effect of his or her "splash." Explain that prayer is like the pebble that creates a ripple effect: Things happen as a result of prayer. In our daily prayer lives, it's important to look for the ripple.

Read the journal entry and share how the prayer was answered. Explain that we often pray for something but never actually pay attention to the answer. When we keep a prayer journal, however, we can go back and look at what we prayed for and see how it was answered. We need to look for the ripple and see how God is answering our prayers. Distribute "Prayer Journal" and pens or pencils and challenge students to keep a prayer journal by spending a few minutes each day praying for the needs of friends, family, missionaries or non-Christians. Allow students five minutes to write their first journal entries as a group. (*Note:* You might want to keep extra copies of "Prayer Journal" on hand at future meetings and invite students to take one as needed.)

Option 2: Let Your Light Shine. For this option, you need a candle and a match. If your meeting room cannot be made fairly dark, make arrangements ahead of time to use a room that can be darkened.

Assemble students in the room, and then turn out the lights. Light the candle and set it in a safe place. Tell students to raise their hands when they are able to see your face as their eyes adjust to the light. After a few moments, everyone should have his or her hand raised.

Explain to the group that it doesn't take much light to see you in the dark room—just a small bit of light can make all the difference. Likewise, the world is a dark place where people can't see the true light. In Matthew 5:14-16, Jesus says that His followers are the light of the world and that we are supposed to let our lights shine in a way that allows others to see God. This means we need to be committed to a personal time of Bible study, prayer and listening to God. We specifically need to be praying for the lost and those who can't see God yet.

Ask the group to pick out one person today whom they know personally and who is not a Christian. Tell them to pray over that person for the next month. This is not a *light* challenge! Give students 30 seconds to pray on their own for that person, then close the time in prayer, asking that God would help us be like Mary and spend time with Him and that He would use us as lights to those around us.

REFLECT

The following short devotions are for the students to reflect on and answer during the week. You can make a copy of these pages and distribute to your class or download and print from **www.gospellight.com/uncommon/jh_ the_new_testament.zip.**

1—UP, UP AND AWAY!

Jam over to James 5:16-18 and get in on the super power.

Imagine you're designing a superhero named "Prayer Warrior." You can choose two of the following for his superhero uniform (check two):

- ❑ Kneepads, so he can pray for hours on end
- ❑ Scotch tape, so he can tape open his eyes when he gets sleepy
- ❑ Nose plugs, so the smell of food won't distract him
- ❑ Gloves, so he won't get his prayer journal dirty
- ❑ Soft-soled shoes, so he can prayer-walk at night without waking anyone
- ❑ Mind-reading glasses, so he can look inside people to find out what they really need prayer for

Well, surprise! Each of us has the chance to be Prayer Warrior. In James 5:16-18, we learn that we can pray for each other for healing and that the prayer of a righteous person (junior-highers included!) can accomplish much. You don't need a superhero uniform; you just need a relationship with God.

Spend a few extra minutes praying for your friends today—especially friends who don't know Christ yet. Be their superhero warrior of prayer!

2—IT'S THAT TIME AGAIN

Before you check your watch, find Hosea 10:12.

Dawn's small-group leader, Carol, had a really cool watch. It was gold and silver and had this really cool black band. Dawn had been admiring it for months when she noticed something strange on it: Carol had put a little green dot sticker on the band. At first, Dawn thought she had put it there on accident, but when she saw Carol the next week at Bible study, she was still wearing it.

Dawn liked the watch so much that she decided to ask Carol, "Why'd you have to ruin the watch by putting the green dot sticker on it?"

The youth leader replied, "Every time I look at the watch and see the sticker, it reminds me to pray and ask God for help in whatever I'm doing."

Suddenly, Dawn began to like that green dot sticker.

Maybe Carol read Hosea 10:12 and found out that no matter what time it is, we can always stop for a moment and pray.

Make a mark on your hand or put a rubber band on your wrist or do something to remind you to stop and spend a few seconds talking with God every time you see it.

3—NOW IS GOOD

If you're wondering when a good time to pray is, check out 1 Thessalonians 5:16-18.

When do you think is the best time to pray?

- ❏ During your church's service
- ❏ While trying to ignore a really boring TV commercial
- ❏ Walking to school
- ❏ While your mom or dad lectures you about your history grade

The truth is that *anytime* is the best time to pray. Paul wrote in 1 Thessalonians 5:16-18 that we are to "pray continually." Maybe you're wondering if that means we should pray in our sleep. Well, that's pretty tricky, so a better idea is to pray as often as we can and look for reminders of God around us.

What is one way you can be reminded of God today? Pray and ask God to help you think about Him today more than you usually do.

4—MAKING INTRODUCTIONS

Skip and hop your way to Acts 2:42-44.

Keith couldn't believe his luck. Just as he is walking into a movie theater with his friends, he literally bumps into Josh, the lead singer of Keith's favorite local band. The group is really popular and plays at all the best Christian parties and local concerts.

Keith introduces himself, and since Josh can tell that Keith is his number-one fan (Keith's forgetting his own name was a clue!), he spends a few minutes talking with him. As Keith turns to go, Josh asks if he wants to grab some ice cream after their movies are over.

Keith ditches his friends after the movie and races to meet Josh. As they enjoy their banana splits, Josh asks Keith why his friends hadn't come with him; they looked like pretty cool people and Josh would have liked to meet them. Keith mumbles something about wanting to spend time with Josh alone and quickly changes the subject.

Being a real friend means that when we meet someone cool, we invite our friends to come along to spend time with the new person. That's what the Early Church members did in Acts 2:42-44; they were constantly introducing others to Jesus through prayer.

Is there someone you can spend time with while you spend time with Jesus today? Maybe you have a friend you can pray with at lunch, thanking God for your food and the day He has given you. Pray and ask God to show you how to pray with someone else today.

THE GENEROUS WIDOW: WHOLEHEARTED GIVING

THE BIG IDEA

We must give from our hearts, not for the purpose of impressing others.

SESSION AIMS

In this session, you will guide students to (1) learn that giving means sharing with others what God has given to us, including Him; (2) feel motivated to trust God by giving back more than what is convenient; and (3) act by identifying tangible ways they can give their abilities, resources or time back to God.

THE BIGGEST VERSE

"They all gave out of their wealth; but she, out of her poverty, put in everything—all she had to live on" (Mark 12:44).

OTHER IMPORTANT VERSES

Genesis 14:20; Numbers 18:26; 1 Samuel 8:15; Mark 12:41-44; Luke 11:42; 2 Corinthians 9:7

Note: Additional options and worksheets in $8^1/_2$" x 11" format for this session are available for download at **www.gospellight.com/uncommon/jh_the_new_testament.zip**.

STARTER

Option 1: The "I Need" Game. For this option, you need candy or other goodies for prizes and a list of items for students to collect. Some item suggestions might be three scrunchies, four socks on each of the runners' hands, five watches attached together, 43 cents, nine shoes tied together, five sweatshirts or sweaters (all worn by the runner), two pairs of glasses, seven earrings, four student ID cards and a $20 bill.

Greet students and divide them into groups of about 10 to 12 each. If your group is small, divide it into two even teams. Explain that you are going to be playing a game called "I Need," and that the winning team will get a prize. Ask each team to select one runner, who will be responsible for bringing you the items you request from his or her team. The first runner in each round who delivers the item to you wins that round and gets a point. Have someone keep score for the teams. Begin the game with a practice round by stating, "I need a piece of gum." (Don't award any points for the practice round.) Play 8 to 10 rounds. After playing the game and awarding the prizes to the winning team, discuss the following:

- Why do people give presents? (*They have to; it's the nice thing to do; it makes others feel good; it makes the person giving the gift feel good.*)
- Have you ever been given a gift, only to be told that you have to share it with someone else? How did you feel about sharing it?
- How do you feel about sharing something that isn't yours, something you've been given to use and care for that belongs to someone else?

To illustrate this last point, share the following scenario:

Imagine that your grandfather had an old train set and he has let you keep it in your room since you were eight years old. Your grandfather enjoyed watching you play with the train set and you enjoyed the responsibility that

Youth Leader Tip

Ask a friend to watch you speak. Get feedback on any quirky sayings or movements you make. Smoothing out your speaking style will remove distractions and allow God's message to ring clearer.

came with taking care of it. You're older now and sometimes you still take it off the shelf and play with it, remembering how much fun you had with your grandfather and the train. Your little brother is now old enough to enjoy the train set and he asks if he can come into your room to play with it.

Ask the group how they would feel about sharing the train with their little brother. Allow for responses, and then transition by stating that God has asked us to take care of His things for Him. He has given His things to care for—not to keep for ourselves. In turn, we are asked to help others by sharing as He does. Today, we're going to check out someone who followed Jesus and understood the importance of giving back to God what He gives to us.

Option 2: Give It Away Relay. For this option, you need two medium trashcans, a source of water and lots of paper cups. Ahead of time, arrange for an outside area to play this game, because it's gonna be a wet one! Place the trashcans approximately 20 feet apart, fill each half full with water, and place an equal amount of paper cups beside each can.

Greet students, and then divide the group into two teams. Explain the rules of the game: Each team's goal is to transfer all of the water in its trashcan to the other team's can by filling paper cups and taking the water over. Players are not allowed to intentionally cause members of the opposing team to spill the water in their cups.

Sounds too easy, doesn't it? The catch is that the water in the cups must be taken over to the opposing team's trashcan by *crabwalking* (walking on one's hands and feet, stomach up)! The cup of water can be placed in a person's mouth, on his or her stomach or in his or her hand; the idea is to spill as little as possible during the transfer. Explain that you will be calling out different instructions for activities other than crabwalking (skipping, running backward, crawling) to transfer the water and that your instructions must be followed immediately.

Play the game for 5-10 minutes. The winning team is the one that has the least amount of water in its trashcan. After the game, discuss the following:

- How did you feel about giving your water to the other team? (*It was easy, because that was the point of the whole game.*)
- What if the water was something that you needed and had worked hard for? How would that change how you felt about giving it away? (*It would have made it harder.*)

- Would it be easier or harder to share something that isn't yours—something you've been given to use and care for that belongs to someone else? Why?

To illustrate this last point, share the following scenario:

Imagine that when you were younger, you really loved Thomas the Tank Engine and Friends. You watched the television show each Saturday morning and knew all of the songs by heart. Your grandfather, knowing how much you loved the show, bought you some wooden tracks and all of the popular characters—Thomas, James, Henry, Gordon, Percy and the rest. He used to love to come over and play trains with you for hours. But now you're older, and, obviously, not as into Thomas as you once were. Sometimes you still take the trains out of the box, as it reminds you of all the fun you used to have with your grandfather, but not that often. Lately, you've noticed that your little brother is really into Thomas. He asks if he can come into your room to play with the set.

Ask the group how they would feel about sharing the train with their little brother. Allow for responses, and then transition to the next step by stating that God has asked us to take care of His things for Him. He has given His things to care for—not to keep for ourselves. In turn, we are asked to help others by sharing as He does. Today, we're going to check out someone who followed Jesus and understood the importance of giving back to God what He gives to us.

MESSAGE

Option 1: Personal Assets. For this option, you need several Bibles, candy or other goodies for prizes, copies of "Personal Assets" (found on the next page) and pens or pencils. Ahead of time, arrange to use a large grass or concrete area or a large empty room where students can spread out to play the game.

Divide the group into two teams and let them know that they'll have a contest to see which team can form four different shapes as you call them out, using every team member for each shape. After creating a shape, a team must wait for your approval before being told the next shape to create. The team that finishes all four shapes first will win a prize. Begin the game by calling out the first shape: a heart. The second shape is a hand; third is a dollar sign; and fourth is Jesus' face.

PERSONAL ASSETS

What do you own? Write a list of things that belong to you.

_____

_____

_____

_____

_____

_____

_____

_____

_____

_____

_____

_____

_____

_____

_____

_____

_____

_____

_____

_____

_____

_____

_____

_____

_____

_____

_____

After awarding the winning team the prizes, reassemble the whole group and explain that today, you are going to be looking at what it means to give from our hearts instead of keeping them back from God by holding on to them for ourselves. Distribute the Bibles and describe the scene from Mark 12:41-44. This scene takes place in the farthest place from the entrance that women were allowed into the Temple, a place called the Court of the Women. (Note that this was called "the Court of the Women" not because there were only women there, but because women could not go beyond this point.) There were 13 trumpet-shaped receptacles for the offerings brought in by the people, and Jesus took a seat where He and His disciples could see the people placing their money into the receptacles. It was a busy day and there were many people placing their offerings. A number of wealthy people were among them, proudly placing large amounts of money into the offering.

Read Mark 12:41-44 aloud, and then explain that the poor widow gave the equivalent of only a few pennies for her offering. It was so little, in fact, that it would have hardly been noticed when it was counted. Jesus took notice, though, and He credited her with giving the greater gift, even though it was the least amount of money given. It was greater than any of the others, because she gave *all that she had* and she gave from her heart. The others gave what was easy and convenient. Giving fully from our heart means giving with an attitude of trusting God and knowing that what we are giving belongs to Him anyway. When we remain comfortable after giving—giving only what is easy to give—we are not trusting God with our gifts.[1]

Distribute "Personal Assets" and pens or pencils and ask students to complete the handout, including anything of value that they consider to be their own (such as an allowance, a savings account, toys, electronics, computers, and the like). Instruct students to circle those items that they would give up right now to someone in need. This is going to be a test of their ability to honestly examine their own heart attitudes.

Give them a few minutes, and then conclude by asking the group, "If God told us to give everything away, could we do it?" State that He probably isn't asking us to give everything we have, but He is asking us to step out in faith and give from our hearts—even if it seems like more than we can afford to give.

Option 2: *The Giving Tree*. For this option, you need several Bibles, the book *The Giving Tree* by Shel Silverstein, copies of "Personal Assets" (found on page 33) and pens or pencils. Read *The Giving Tree* aloud, making sure students can see the illustrations. After reading the book, discuss the following:

- What made the tree happy? (*Giving to the boy.*)
- At what point did the tree appear sad? (*When she thought she had nothing left to give.*)

Distribute Bibles and describe the scene from Mark 12:41-44: This scene takes place in the farthest place from the entrance that women were allowed into the Temple, a place called the Court of the Women. (Note that this was called "the Court of the Women" not because there were only women there, but because women could not go beyond this point.) There were 13 trumpet-shaped receptacles for the offerings brought in by the people, and Jesus took a seat where He and His disciples could see the people placing their money into the receptacles. It was a busy day and there were many people placing their offerings. A number of wealthy people were among them, proudly placing large amounts of money into the offering.

Read Mark 12:41-44. Note to the group that the woman in the story put in *two mites.* Today, this would be the equivalent to only a few pennies. Compared to the large sums put in by the rich people, this would seem to be a very insignificant amount. But Jesus didn't think so. In fact, He credited her with giving the greater gift, even though it was the least amount of money given.

Now discuss the following questions:

- Why do you think Jesus considered hers the greater gift? (*Because the widow gave from her heart and gave all that she had, while others gave only what was convenient or easy.*)

- If she was so poor, why would she have given so much to the Temple offering? (*Because her heart attitude was right and she knew that all she had already belonged to God. She knew He would use what she gave for His glory and that He would provide the things she needed.*)

- What about the people who gave a lot of money, why didn't their gifts count as much? (*Their offerings may have been worth more in worldly terms, but what they gave didn't require them to trust God. They didn't give from resources necessary for their survival. They were wealthy; their offerings were easy and convenient to give.*)

Distribute "Personal Assets" and pens or pencils. Ask the students to complete the handout, including anything of value that they consider to be their own (such as an allowance, savings, toys, electronics, computers, and so forth). Instruct students to circle those items that they would give up right now to someone in need. This is going to be a test of their ability to examine their own heart attitudes.

Give them a few minutes to complete the handout, and then discuss what kind of trust it would take for them to give away everything they just listed for God. How about giving up their bedroom or their parents' support? If God asked them to give *everything* away, could they do it? Explain that God probably isn't going to ask us to give *everything* we have, but He is asking us to step out in faith and give from our hearts, even if it seems like more than we can afford to give.

Conclude by stating that the widow gave all that she had, and she gave it from her heart. When we give from our hearts, it is with an attitude of trusting God and knowing that what we are giving is really His anyway. When we remain comfortable, holding on to what we believe is ours, we are not trusting God with our lives.

DIG

Option 1: A.R.T. For this option, you need several Bibles, a whiteboard and a dry-erase marker, blank pieces of paper and pens or pencils.

Distribute the paper and pens or pencils and ask students to draw self-portraits on the fronts of their papers and then write their names on the backs. Allow two minutes for drawing; then collect all the pictures. One at a time, show the pictures to the whole group and ask if anyone can guess who the artist is.

Explain that an artist's self-portrait, whether simple or detailed, cannot possibly give us a complete picture of the artist. Right now, we're going to talk about art in a different sense—as an acronym for three attributes we all possess. Write the following on the whiteboard:

A = ABILITIES (things we can do)
R = RESOURCES (things we have)
T = TIME (use of our time)

Tell the group that using this acronym as a guideline, today we're going to get a more complete picture of what we are able to give God. Return the self-portraits to students. Ask them to turn the page over to the back and write the letters *A*, *R* and *T* down the left side of the page with space between each letter. Have them write beside each letter the gifts God has given them that they can use to serve Him. For example, an *ability* might be singing, a *resource* might be a swimming pool, and *time* would be any particular time that students typically have during a day or week when they could serve God. Allow five minutes for students to complete their ART lists, and then ask for ideas from their lists to write on the whiteboard.

Once you have several suggestions for each of the three areas, ask students to brainstorm ways in which those ideas could be used to serve God. When you're sure students are on the right track, ask them to write down three or four ideas on their self-portraits for ways to serve God using their own unique gifts.

Option 2: An A.R.T. Case Study. For this option, you need a whiteboard and a dry-erase marker. Read the following story:

> Tanya lives in the suburbs of Chicago. Her dad is a contractor and her mom is a full-time homemaker. Tanya has three younger siblings; her brother is eight and her sisters are five and two. She really enjoys taking care of her two-year-old sister, Emily.
>
> Tanya gets a weekly allowance of $10 (which she usually spends on music downloads or nail polish). She sings in her school choir and plays on the soccer team. She loves animals, especially dogs, and has a golden retriever named Ralph. Whenever she has time, Tanya likes to experiment with new and interesting recipes for baking cookies. Her favorite so far is an oatmeal cookie with blueberries instead of raisins.
>
> While Tanya was at youth group last weekend, the pastor challenged students to find ways they can give back to God from the things He has given them. But Tanya doesn't feel like she has anything to offer God.

After reading the story, discuss the following with the group:

- What are some of Tanya's abilities? (*Singing, cooking, playing soccer and likes animals and kids.*)
- What are some of her resources? (*Ten dollars per week, a dad who builds stuff, a mom who is available to help; she also has a house, siblings and a dog.*)
- What is her availability? How much time does she have to give? (*It depends on her desire to give.*)

- What are some of the ways Tanya can give back to God? (*Some possible ideas: She could give a dollar a week to her church offering or skip buying an item regularly and sponsor a needy child. She could sing in retirement homes or give kids voice lessons. She could walk neighborhood dogs for free. She could bake cookies to give to the new neighbors who just moved in down the street. She could baby-sit free of charge for families that can't afford a babysitter.*)

Write the following on the whiteboard:

A = ABILITIES (things we can do)
R = RESOURCES (things we have)
T = TIME (use of our time)

Have students think of a few things they have to offer back to God based on their abilities, resources and time. Write some of their suggestions on the whiteboard and point out ideas that require time. Remind students that they may need to cut some things out of their already busy schedules in order to be able to give their time to God.

APPLY

Option 1: Make a Pledge. For this option, you need copies of "Pledge Worksheet" (found on the next page), pens or pencils, and an offering basket or plate (if you want to be informal, baseball caps do just fine).

Ask who in the group knows the Pledge of Allegiance. After waiting for the responses, discuss what it means to make a pledge. Explain that a pledge is a binding promise to do or give or to refrain from doing something.

Now ask the group what is a tithe. (Note that a tithe literally means "10," but it generally refers to giving 10 percent of one's income.) Continue by stating

Youth Leader Tip
Provide opportunities for students to use their gifts to serve God by serving others. Students can sing at a retirement home, write to needy kids, provide a pool for a youth gathering or work together to sponsor a child.

PLEDGE WORKSHEET

How much money do you usually receive during a month?

Money Source	Amount	10 Percent (Amount x .01)
Allowance		
Chores		
Babysitting		
Job		
Mowing lawns		
Paper route		
Washing cars		
Gifts		
Total		

I pledge to give God 10 percent of the income that I receive through my allowance and other ways of earning income. I pledge to give $ _____ each month to support my church and the work that it is doing to further God's kingdom.

_____

Signature

_____

Date

that tithes are our gifts to God. In the Old Testament, a tithe meant 10 percent of a person's income. When people tithed, they sacrificially gave their "first fruits"—the *first* 10 percent of their income.

Distribute "Pledge Worksheet" and pens or pencils, and instruct students to use the handouts to figure out 10 percent of their monthly income from allowance, chores, babysitting, yard work, and so forth. Explain that the 10-percent figure they end up with is their tithe. Challenge students to give that amount each month to God. For some, it may prove difficult to let go of their money. Those who find it difficult should ask God to help them give for just two months—they will be pleasantly surprised by how He provides for their needs.

Continue by telling the students that if they want to give more than 10 percent of their income—they should go for it! We are told in 2 Corinthians 9:7 that God loves a cheerful giver. Conclude by instructing students to fill out and sign their pledge cards, tear them in half, place the top half into the offering basket and keep the bottom half as a reminder of their commitment to give.

Option 2: Penny Wise. For this option, you need a copy of "Big Cents" (found on the next page) for every four students, pens or pencils, and several containers to put the "pennies" in (such as bowls, buckets or baseball caps). Ahead of time, cut the handouts into four sections each.

Distribute "Big Cents" and remind students that although junior-highers don't usually have a lot of *money,* they each have loads of *talents* that are just as valuable. Ask them to write their name and one talent God has given them that they could use to serve, and then write the names of individuals or groups that they could serve with their talents on their "penny."

Divide students into groups of three to five and give each group a container. Explain that just like the widow's offering, these pennies are a chance for them to give back to God and others at the same time. Instruct students to share what their gifts are one at a time within their small group and then place their "penny" in the containers. Keep the pennies and follow up later by asking students if they have been able to give their talents to serve someone.

BIG CENTS

REFLECT

The following short devotions are for the students to reflect on and answer during the week. You can make a copy of these pages and distribute to your class or download and print from **www.gospellight.com/uncommon/jh_ the_new_testament.zip.**

1—SPARE NO EXPENSE

Grab that Bible near you and read Proverbs 21:25-26.

Uh, oh, you think to yourself, *Dorena is at it again!* It seems like every day Dorena forgets to bring notebook paper to school and has to walk around before English class, asking if she can borrow some paper from someone. Of course, it's not actually *borrowing* because she never pays anyone back. As Dorena approaches you with her need, you respond by . . .

- ❑ Waving a piece of paper in her face and yelling, "No way!"
- ❑ Wadding up a piece of paper and throwing it at her head, knowing she won't be able to use it.
- ❑ Ignoring her.
- ❑ Pointing out how she could save a lot of trees by writing her notes on her arms.
- ❑ Giving her three pieces of paper, just in case she needs more later.

Proverbs 21:25-26 encourages us to give "without sparing," even when we don't want to. Today, try to find two people that you can give something to, anything from a candy bar to a dollar. You'll hardly miss it, and you'll be glad that you had the chance to share with someone. Spend a few minutes asking God to help you do this, because when you actually have the chance to give something away, it might be harder than you think!

2—NOT OPTIONAL

If you like gifts, race over to Romans 12:6-8.

Whew! Ronnie breathed a sigh of relief after he read Romans 12:6-8. He had felt bad because he wasn't giving money to the church or to people who needed it, but now he has a way out. He only has to give if he has the spiritual gift of giving, which he is absolutely sure he doesn't. He can keep *everything* to himself!

Ronnie comes to share his joyous discovery with you. What would you tell him? Hopefully, you would tell Ronnie that giving isn't only a spiritual gift; it's part of being obedient to Christ. Everyone is supposed to give, but some people who have the gift of giving are probably better at it and do more of it.

Are you giving your tithe (10 percent of all of your money) to God? If not, repent and ask God to help you start giving. If so, ask God if there is anything else He would like you to give—maybe even today.

3—NEED SOME REFRESHMENT?

What are you waiting for? Flip open to Proverbs 11:24-25.

Dominique just couldn't believe what she was seeing. She and 13 other junior-highers from her church were on a missions trip to Mexico, helping Amelia and Juan and their three kids build a new home. Their old house was about as big as Dominique's bedroom, and all five members of the family had been living in it. Amelia and Juan had no refrigerator, and each of them owned just a few outfits each. Dominique had felt sorry for them when she first met them.

But when Dominique saw their faces, she didn't feel sorry for them anymore. In fact, she was in awe as she realized that Amelia and Juan felt blessed to give what little they had. You see, they had decided to make fresh, homemade tamales for all 14 junior-highers. Dominique realized that, because Amelia and Juan only had a limited amount of food, feeding her and her friends would mean that their family would not have much to eat later in the week . . . but they didn't seem to care! They were all smiles and kept saying how happy they were to be eating together. Dominique knew that her own parents wouldn't be quite so happy if they had to feed so many people at such a great cost to themselves.

Dominique was seeing Proverbs 11:24-25 in action. Giving brings God's blessings, and although this at times *might* mean more money, more often it means joy and peace.

Is your giving refreshing you? If not, maybe you're not doing it enough or you're doing it with the wrong attitude.

Ask God to help you know what you need to give away this week.

4—PAY IT BACK

Stop reading this and start reading Romans 13:7.

You breathe a sigh of relief when Gilbert walks the other way. Last week you needed lunch money and he loaned you four dollars. Now every time you see him, you feel a little bit guilty about it. In fact, you actually have the money to pay him back in your pocket, but you're hoping that he'll forget about it and you'll get to keep the money.

Paul's words in Romans 13:7 should change your mind. We are to give back whatever we owe to people. Do you owe anybody money today? If so, search your pockets, backpack, wallet or purse and find the money, so you can pay them back.

ZACK ATTACK: WHOLEHEARTED SURRENDER

THE BIG IDEA

Jesus wants a relationship with us and calls us to make radical changes to follow Him.

SESSION AIMS

In this session you will guide students to (1) learn that Jesus wants them to be found; (2) experience the joy that comes from salvation; and (3) act by identifying one way they can share their joy with another person this week.

THE BIGGEST VERSE

"For the Son of Man came to seek and to save what was lost" (Luke 19:10).

OTHER IMPORTANT VERSES

Numbers 5:5-10; Matthew 20:1-16; Luke 5:29-32; John 14:6; Romans 1:18-20; Ephesians 2:8-9

Note: Additional options and worksheets in 8$^1/_2$" x 11" format for this session are available for download at **www.gospellight.com/uncommon/jh_the_new_testament.zip**.

STARTER

Option 1: Find Me! For this option, you'll need enough blindfolds for each student to have one (bandanas, old T-shirts or strips of cloth work well) and a prize (candy or another goody).

As students arrive, divide them into pairs and distribute the blindfolds. Ask the pairs to decide on a pair of words that go together as their password, such as "peanut butter," "video game," "skate board," and so forth. Each partner will choose one of the words as his or her personal password (i.e., one partner's password would be "peanut" and the other's password would be "butter").

Instruct one person in each pair to go to the opposite side of the room. Have all of the students put on the blindfolds while you explain the rules of the game. The object is for each pair to reunite from across the room by repeating their personal passwords. For example, one partner would say "peanut" and his or her partner would answer "butter." The difficulty will be in listening for only their partners' word while trying to tune out all the other passwords being called out! Students will walk across the room, saying their passwords until they find their partners. The first pair to reunite wins the prize.

After the game, discuss the following:

- What made it difficult to be reunited with your partner? (*You couldn't see; there was a lot of other noise.*)
- What did you need to do in order to reunite with your partner? (*You needed to listen for your partner's word while continuing to repeat your own word for your partner to hear.*)
- At any point, did anyone feel lost? Were any of you lost as a small child? How did you feel while you were lost? (*Worried, scared, fun, didn't care.*)
- How did you reunite with your parents? What was your reaction when you were found? What was your parents' reaction?

Explain that if someone were really lost, he or she would probably feel worried and scared. Today, we will be studying a lesser-known follower of Jesus who was separated from Him, and how Jesus found him.

Option 2: Search and Rescue. For this option, you need at least five brave adult volunteers (you'll need more than the number of student teams you anticipate) and candy or other goodies for a prize.

Ahead of time, arrange for the volunteers to be "lost victims" in a game of Search and Rescue. They should hide in places around the church campus or meeting area where they will be difficult to find but not difficult to access. Let the volunteers know that they should pretend to be hurt and allow themselves to be rescued by being carried from their hiding places to the meeting room.

Greet students and divide them into teams of 7 to 10 students each. Explain that you are going to play a game of Search and Rescue, and each team's goal is to find "lost victims." Each successful rescue is worth 150 points. When a team finds a lost victim, the victim needs to be transported back to the safety of the meeting room. Teams can travel together or in smaller groups; however, if a smaller group finds a victim and there are not enough team members to lift the victim and carry him or her, another team can steal the victim. Once a victim is lifted from the ground, he/she cannot touch the ground again until he/she reaches the meeting room or the team transporting him/her will only be credited with half the points (75) for that rescue.

After the game (approximately 15 to 20 minutes), award the prize to the team with the most rescue points. Next, ask the whole group the following questions:

- Were any of you ever lost as a small child?
- How did you feel while you were lost?
- How did you reunite with your parents?

Conclude by stating that today, we're going to learn about a lesser-known follower of Christ who found out how to be reunited with Jesus.

MESSAGE

Option 1: Zacchaeus Melodrama. For this option, you need several Bibles and prizes for six brave volunteers.

Distribute the Bibles. Explain that today you're going to learn another story from the life of Jesus. Remind students that each "short story"—such as the story

Youth Leader Tip
Video clips are a great way for you to grab your students' attention. Create video announcements, videotape interviews or use clips during your message. This will enhance your students' memory.

of Martha and Mary or of the widow with two pennies—is an episode in the "big story" of Jesus' life, ministry, death and resurrection. His big story is recorded in the four New Testament Gospels, and while sometimes people think the Bible is boring, today we are going to see that it doesn't need to be. Ask for six volunteers to help demonstrate how fun the Bible can really be, and then assign the following six parts: Zacchaeus, a sycamore-fig tree, Jesus and three onlookers. Explain that as you read Luke 19:1-10 aloud, the volunteers will act out their roles, taking their cues from what you read. Read the passage, pausing at appropriate times for the actors to act out their roles.

After you've read the passage, applaud the impromptu performance, reward the actors with prizes and invite them to return to their seats. Discuss the following questions:

- Why do you think Zacchaeus wanted to see Jesus so badly? (*He was curious and wanted to know if what he was hearing was true. He was probably wondering if Jesus was the Messiah and if Jesus could help him.*)

- What was Zacchaeus's response when Jesus called him? (*He came down rejoicing. He was as excited as a lost child who finds his or her parents.*)

- Zacchaeus was a rich man, but he probably didn't have many friends because of his job as a tax collector. Do you think he may have felt lost? (*Maybe. He was definitely looking for something, as evidenced by his climbing the tree to see Jesus. Zacchaeus was lost because of the sin in his life and he needed Jesus' forgiveness. Jesus found Zacchaeus and showed him love by being a guest in his house. Zacchaeus listened to Jesus, turned from his sin and was forgiven.*)[1]

Option 2: Celebrity Guest. For this option, you need several Bibles, an adult volunteer (preferably one who's well known to students), and a soft ball appropriate for tossing indoors.

Ahead of time, think of a personal story of something you lost (such as a pet, a piece of jewelry, a toy, your wallet), ideally something you really liked or loved, either from your childhood or recently. It can be corny or sentimental; it's up to you. Arrange for the volunteer to enter the room just as you finish your story, and excitedly whisper something into your ear.

Begin telling the story about your loss, describing the effort you put into finding the lost item. If you eventually found it, describe how you felt. Be sure to dramatize the situation as much as possible.

When you are finished, the adult volunteer should rush into the room and whisper something into your ear. Look surprised and ask, "Are you sure? Are you *really* sure?" Allow him or her to reassure you, and then notify the students that a well-known actor (use a specific name) is visiting an uncle who attends the church and the actor is on his or her way to your church. Chances are students will react by saying, "No way. That's not true." But at least some (if not most) will believe you, and when you suggest that they run to the window (or a nearby door—wherever is appropriate) to try to see the famous church guest, you can expect a stampede. Of course, the famous actor won't be seen, and after a few moments you'll need to let students know the truth.

Apologize for fooling the students, and then explain you did so for a good reason, as they will see in today's lesson about Zacchaeus. He was so excited about seeing Jesus that he actually climbed a tree just to get a glimpse of Him.

Distribute the Bibles. Explain that today you're going to learn another story from the life of Jesus. Remind students that each "short story"—such as the story of Martha and Mary or of the widow with two pennies—is an episode in the "big story" of Jesus' life, ministry, death and resurrection. His big story is recorded in the four New Testament Gospels. Ask students to find Luke 19:1-10. Read verse 1 and toss the ball to a student. Have him or her read verse 2, and then toss the ball to someone else, who will read verse 3. Continue this until all 10 verses have been read. Explain that Jesus was known as a friend of tax collectors (see Luke 5:29-32; 7:34), but Zacchaeus was probably wealthy, and Jesus made it clear that it was tough for wealthy people to enter into heaven (see Luke 18:18-25). Yet Zacchaeus went to some pretty drastic lengths to see Jesus.

- Why do you think Zacchaeus wanted to see Jesus so badly? (*He was probably curious and wanted to know if what he was hearing was true. He was probably wondering if Jesus was the Messiah and if Jesus could help him.*)

- What was Zacchaeus's response when Jesus called him? (*He came down rejoicing. He was as excited as a lost child who finds his or her parents.*)

- Zacchaeus was a rich man, but he probably didn't have many friends because of his job as a tax collector. Do you think he may have felt lost? (*Maybe. He was definitely looking for something, as evidenced by his climbing the tree to see Jesus. Zacchaeus was lost because of the sin in his life and he needed Jesus' forgiveness. Jesus found Zacchaeus and showed him love by being a guest in his house. Zacchaeus listened to Jesus, turned from his sin and was forgiven.*)

Conclude by stating that it was the sin in Zacchaeus's life that made him lost. When he turned from his sin, he was found and forgiven by Jesus.

DIG

Option 1: Uninvited Guest. For this option, you need nothing, zip, nada. Read the following story:

Zack is a foul-mouthed bully that nobody likes at school. He constantly annoys everyone sitting near him in class by taking their pens, notebooks, pencil boxes—anything he can get his hands on. At lunch, he cuts in front of people in line and runs into people on purpose, causing them to spill food everywhere. Zack is always teasing the Christians at school, calling them "squares" and "Jesus freaks." Most students keep their distance from Zack, making fun of him behind his back.

One night Zack shows up at an event at your church. When your friends see him, they start grumbling and complaining, "Why is *he* here? He belongs in jail, not in our church!" Their rude comments continue as you notice that Zack is sitting in the back row by himself and not one person in the youth group has welcomed him.

Now ask the group the following questions:

- Does anyone know someone like Zack? (*A simple yes or no works well here. Don't allow students to use this as an opportunity to gossip.*)
- What do you think would happen if that person came to this group? (*He or she would probably be rejected.*)
- Why do you think that would happen? (*People like Zack are troublemakers and won't be perceived as being "deserving" of being accepted by the group.*)
- Does anyone here sin as badly as Zack? (*No way!*)

Continue by stating that given this, it would seem that we don't have to worry about our sin as much as Zack because he is much worse than us. Right? Well, guess what? Sin is sin. Period. As Paul wrote in Romans 3:23, "All have sinned and fall short of the glory of God." It doesn't matter how big or little we think our sin is. The consequences might be different here on earth, but it's all the same in the eyes of God when it comes to our salvation.

Ask the group whether, based on Romans 3:23, Zack would deserve God's grace less than you or me. The answer is of course not: God says we are saved by grace, which is a gift that isn't earned or deserved. It is not a result of anything we do, but a result of what Jesus did on the cross for us (see Ephesians 2:8-9). If we come to Him and accept His gift of salvation—the gift of His paying the price of our sins for us on the cross—we are saved and will be with Him forever.

Conclude by stating that in Romans 10:9, Paul says, "If you confess with your mouth 'Jesus is Lord,' and believe in your heart that God raised him from the dead, you will be saved." Once we receive Jesus' forgiveness, we are forgiven forever for our previous sins. The result of this should be our total desire to follow Jesus and His plan for us to live righteous lives. That doesn't mean we don't continue to sin along the way. We will always sin, but if we ask His forgiveness when we do, we are forgiven. Our goal, however, is to follow Jesus because we're so grateful that He's saved us.

Option 2: Sin-O-Meter. For this option, you need copies of "Sin-O-Meter" (found on the next page) and pens or pencils.

Distribute "Sin-O-Meter" and pens or pencils and ask students to rank the sins listed on the handout and write them in on the "Sin-O-Meter." Allow time to complete the handout, and then survey how students ranked the sins listed.

Discuss with the group whether they think someone who commits murder would deserve to go to heaven. (*The answer will be no.*) Ask if anyone there has sinned as bad as that. (*Expect a resounding "no!"*) Given this, it would seem that we don't have to worry about our sin as much as a murderer does. Right? *Wrong.* To God, sin is sin. In Romans 3:23, Paul wrote, "All have sinned and fall short of the glory of God." What we consider little sins are no different than big sins when it comes to being with God.

Explain that while it's certain that different sins will have different consequences here on earth, to God *any sin* means separation from Him. If we don't

Youth Leader Tip

Breaking into small groups can be stressful, but is also an opportunity to build community. Take the stress out by using colored markers to mark the hands of students as they arrive, designating groups by color.

SIN-O-METER

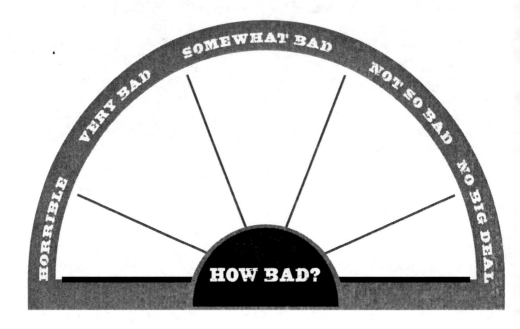

Rank the following sins by writing them in the above Sin-O-Meter:

Stealing candy	Stealing a car
Gossiping	Hijacking a plane
Speeding	Cheating on a test
Ditching school	Killing someone
Using drugs	Talking back to parents
Lying	Being mean
Robbing a bank	Getting drunk
Beating someone up	Graffiti on a wall

know Jesus and commit only *little* sins, we won't receive eternal life. If we have committed *big* sins, but we now know Jesus, we are heaven-bound. What? Does this mean that a mass murderer who finds Jesus gets to go to heaven while our dear Aunt Sadie, a sweet little old lady who doesn't know Jesus but has never hurt anyone in her life, goes to *hell?* Why?

Explain that God says that we are saved by *grace*, which is a gift that isn't earned or deserved. It is not a result of anything we do but a result of what Jesus did on the cross for us (see Ephesians 2:8-9). If we come to Him and accept His gift—that He paid the price of our sin for us on the cross—we are saved and will go to heaven.

In Romans 10:9, Paul teaches, "If you confess with your mouth, 'Jesus is Lord,' and believe in your heart that God raised him from the dead, you will be saved." Once we receive Jesus' forgiveness, we are forgiven forever for our previous sins. The result of this should be our total desire to follow Jesus and His plan for us to live righteous lives. That doesn't mean we don't continue to sin along the way. We will always sin, but if we ask His forgiveness when we do, we are forgiven. Our goal, however, is to follow Jesus because we're so grateful that He's saved us.

So what about other people who we think sin worse than us? Explain that the truth is that we are all equal when it comes to needing God's grace. Rather than pointing fingers at people, we should be pointing people to Jesus.

APPLY

Option 1: Empty-Seat Challenge. For this option, you need copies of "Empty-Seat Challenge" (found on the next page), pens or pencils and a chair.

Place the chair deliberately in front of the students, explaining that it's time to share their joy about being found by Jesus with people who haven't been found yet. The chair represents an empty space to be filled by someone who has yet to know Jesus. Move the chair, place it in the middle of the group and ask students to think about a non-Christian friend or family member who could fill the empty seat. Encourage them to begin praying for the person they are thinking about, asking that God would begin to soften his or her heart to have the desire to know Jesus when he or she hears about Him.

Distribute "Empty Seat-Challenge" and pens or pencils, and then ask students to write the name of the person they are going to pray for on the handout. Invite them to take their handouts home and keep them on their mirrors or desks as a reminder to pray for that person and invite him or her to the

Empty-Seat Challenge

On the chairs below, write the name of someone you know who doesn't know Jesus yet—someone you would like to invite to take an empty seat in your youth ministry soon. Remember that writing his or her name means you're committed to praying for that person!

youth group. Close in prayer, praying for all people who will someday sit in the empty chair.

Option 2: Mind the Gap. For this option, you need several gift Bibles, a whiteboard and a dry-erase marker. Inform students that today, you're going to give them an opportunity to begin a relationship with God right now, right this minute. Draw two vertical lines on the whiteboard with a gap in between. Write "you" on the left side, "God" on the right side and "sin" at the bottom of the gap. It should look something like this:

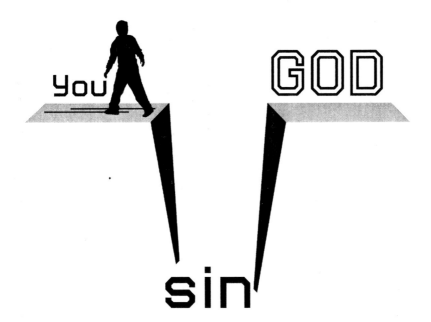

Explain to the group that because of our sin, there is an unbridgeable gap between us and God. We can't get to God on our own. Being good doesn't help us cross it, being religious doesn't help us cross it—nothing we do gets us to God. But because God wants to have a relationship with us, He sent His Son, Jesus, to make a way. Jesus lived a perfect life—the only person, in fact, ever to live that never sinned—yet He was put to death on a cross to pay the price owed for all of our sins. He died for us. Three days later, God raised Him from the dead, beating death and paying for our sins. Now we have a bridge so we can get to God.

Draw a cross in the middle of the gap, making a bridge from one side to the other. Write "Jesus" across the cross.

State that from Jesus' own words in John 14:6, we learn that Jesus is the way back to God. Jesus paid for our sins, and we are saved from eternal separation from God if we simply ask Jesus into our life. Yet there is a cost: Jesus wants our lives. He wants us to follow Him. We are forgiven and He won't ever leave us, but He wants us to respond by turning from our ways and following Him.

Ask students to bow their heads and close their eyes. Invite all who want a relationship with God and who desire His loving forgiveness to pray along with you as you pray the following aloud:

> *God, I know that I am a sinner. Thank You that Jesus died so that I can have a relationship with You. I want Your forgiveness. Take my life, God, and help me to follow You. Amen.*

Invite all who prayed that prayer with you to raise their hands (or raise their heads to look at you). Make a mental note of those who prayed the prayer with you and encourage them to let others know about the exciting decision they just made. Explain that everyone in the group wants to support and help them in this new journey they've begun.

Ask those who said that prayer asking Jesus into their hearts to come forward. Encourage all who come forward by clapping for them or hugging them. Present each of them with a gift Bible, and invite them to stay after the session so that you can answer any questions they might have. Be sure to get names, phone numbers and email addresses if you don't already have them, so you can follow up later in the week. (*Note:* Following up within one week is the key to helping new believers grow in their faith.)

REFLECT

The following short devotions are for the students to reflect on and answer during the week. You can make a copy of these pages and distribute to your class or download and print from **www.gospellight.com/uncommon/jh_ the_new_testament.zip.**

1—LIKE A CHILD

If you like little kids (and even if you don't), make your way to Matthew 18:1-4.

Megan has come to you feeling really worried. Her twin sister, Erin, came home from last week's Bible study on Matthew 18 and started to change. Although you missed the Bible study and had no idea what Matthew 18 was about, you are surprised as she tells you that Erin has started sucking her thumb and sleeping with her teddy bear. At night she even wears flannel pajamas with little footies in them.

You figure that if you are going to help Erin, you should read Matthew 18. As soon as you finish, you realize the problem. Erin's problem is that she thinks that Jesus was talking about *acting* like a child instead of being humble like a child. Oops!

Shine a flashlight into your own life to see if there is any pride in there and take a few minutes to confess it to God. Ask Him to make you as humble as a little kid (and, no, that doesn't mean you have to wear flannel pajamas with footies in them).

2—DON'T SPILL!

Race to Luke 5:36-39 and see if you can get there first.

Which spill would be the hardest to clean up?

- ❑ Grape juice on the white couch
- ❑ Ice cream in your sister's hair (don't ask)
- ❑ Chocolate syrup puddled on brown carpet
- ❑ Ink from a blue pen on blue jeans nearly the same color

The truth is that none of them would be very fun to clean up, but the one that would probably prove the most difficult would be the grape juice. If you were the one cleaning up, you wouldn't want grape juice to spill—and neither would Jesus.

In Luke 5:36-39, Jesus talked about new wine spilling. This was a real problem when new wine was poured into old wineskins—the old skins often broke open and spilled the new wine all over the place. In the same way, when Jesus does new things in your life, He wants you to change along the way. He wants you to be a new wineskin, securely holding what He has poured into you.

Are there any habits you have that are keeping you from Him? It could be cheating, looking at Internet porn, gossiping or something else. Chances are that only you and God know about it. Take a few minutes to confess it to Him and ask God to help you run away from it, to become the new wineskin He wants you to be.

3—STITCHED TOGETHER

If you like new things, check out 2 Corinthians 5:17-21.

Jon raced after school to meet his friends and play touch football in the park a few blocks from his house. Usually he went home first to change from his nicer shirt to one he kept for football, but today he didn't have time, since he had to stay a little late in P.E. to help the coach clean up the softball equipment.

The game went great. Jon made a couple of really good catches, and his team won 17 to 14. Over dinner, as Jon was telling his family about his game, his stepdad asked him what had happened to his shirt. Jon looked over and was bummed when he saw a hole about the size of two quarters over his right elbow. It must have happened when he played defense and tried to grab the other team's running back.

Before Jon had a chance to get too sad about it, his stepdad asked him to take off the shirt so he could sew it back together. Luckily, his stepdad had done some minor sewing on uniforms when he was in the Marines, and in just a matter of minutes, he handed the shirt back to Jon, who couldn't believe his eyes . . . it looked as good as new!

The truth is that more than our shirts are ruined until we know Jesus. Before we come to know Christ, our entire life is ripped and tattered. He comes and sews us up, making us new creations. Today, spend some extra time thanking God for making you a new creation and for all the people He put in your life to help you learn about Him.

If you want to know the kind of changes that really matter, blitz to Galatians 6:12-18.

If you were trying to annoy your non-Christian friends with the fact that you are a Christian, which would be the most obnoxious?

- ❑ Wearing a T-shirt every day that listed their names and the fact that they are going to hell
- ❑ Putting John 3:16 bumper stickers on their lockers and book covers
- ❑ Singing hymns as you walk around the halls with them

It's hard to pick which is the most obnoxious because they're all pretty annoying. When the apostle Paul, the author of most of the New Testament letters, wrote that circumcision (the traditional way Jews identified themselves as God's people) was unnecessary for Christians, he was encouraging people to look beyond outward appearances to the hearts of people. He exclaims, "What really counts is a new creation."

How can people see your heart—the heart that has been changed by Jesus—today? How can you share all He has done for you? Ask God to show you how and to give you courage to use the opportunities He gives you. It's almost guaranteed He will provide some for you today!

THE CENTURION: A TRUSTING FAITH

THE BIG IDEA

We demonstrate our faith when we bring our needs to God and trust Him to care for us.

SESSION AIMS

In this session, you will guide students to (1) learn they can have faith in Jesus' power; (2) feel peace and assurance that they don't have to meet their needs on their own; and (3) show their faith by bringing a specific need to God.

THE BIGGEST VERSE

"But say the word, and my servant will be healed" (Luke 7:7).

OTHER IMPORTANT VERSES

Psalm 55:22; Mark 9:14-27; Luke 7:1-10; John 14:27; 18:15-18,25-27; Hebrews 11:1; James 1:2-4

Note: Additional options and worksheets in 8$^1/_2$" x 11" format for this session are available for download at **www.gospellight.com/uncommon/jh_the_new_testament.zip**.

STARTER

Option 1: You've Got to Have Faith. For this option, you need a whiteboard and a dry-erase marker (or butcher paper taped to the wall and a felt-tip pen), blank notepaper, pens or pencils, and candy or other goodies for prizes.

Greet students and divide them into teams of five or six. (For groups of less than 10, divide them into pairs.) Explain that every day we put our faith in lots of things. For example, have them consider the clothes they're wearing right now. Each of us has faith that our clothes are not going to disintegrate and leave us standing in front of each other in our underwear. After the giggling subsides, distribute a sheet of blank paper to each team and pens or pencils, and ask teams to come up with a list of physical things they have put their faith in during the last week (such as cars, chairs or skateboards). The team that comes up with the most items will get a prize.

Explain that there's a catch, however (surprise, surprise!). Items will *only* count toward their team's score if another team hasn't written the same item on their list. If two or more groups have the same item, that item doesn't count. That means groups will have to be creative and think of unusual things that they have had faith in during the last seven days. (Note that naming people also doesn't count.)

Allow four or five minutes of brainstorming. As the teams work, draw columns on the whiteboard, one for each team. When time is up, ask teams to, one at a time, share their lists. Ask for a volunteer to write down each team's items on the whiteboard. Have each team share its ideas and how each item is trusted. When each team has offered its list, cross off repeats and tally up the totals, awarding a prize to the winning team.

Now discuss the following questions:

- Imagine you've never seen or heard of a parachute, but a professional skydiver comes to you and asks you to jump out of a plane with him. What's your response? (*Are you crazy?! Do you want me to die?!*)

- How could the professional skydiver help you have faith that it is okay to jump from the plane? (*Tell me about the parachute; show me how a parachute works; give me safety statistics; jump and show that it really does work.*)

- After you have heard the statistics and seen what the parachute does, do you think you would be more likely to jump? (*Probably.*)

- What if the professional skydiver jumped, but his parachute didn't work. Would you be inclined to jump right behind him? Why or why not? (*No way! I wouldn't have faith that the parachute would stop my fall unless I saw that it worked successfully.*)

Transition to the next step by explaining that whether it's a parachute or our clothing, we have to believe something will work in order to have faith in it. The same is true about having faith in people. Today, we're going to check out someone who had more faith that Jesus' power would work than Jesus had ever seen before.

Option 2: Blind Faith. For this option, you need one adult volunteer for every 8 to 10 students, several blindfolds, candy or other goodies for prizes, items for an obstacle course (such as traffic cones, trashcans, chairs, ramps) and lots of room! Set up the obstacle course ahead of time. Make sure it's challenging, but not too difficult to get through. You will want students to succeed at navigating this course.

Greet students and divide them into teams of 8 to 10. Assign each team an adult who is the official "blindfold bandit" and give that person several blindfolds. The blindfold bandit should blindfold at least three of the stronger students on each team. Each of the blindfolded students should find a teammate, ideally someone who is lighter than he or she is. Explain that when you say go, the blindfolded team member will carry his or her teammate through the obstacle course. When they return, the next pair can start the course. As each pair returns, they should give their blindfold to the blindfold bandit so that it can be tied on one member of another pair waiting to complete the course. Each team member must go through the obstacle course, either as a carrier or a rider. The team that gets everyone through the obstacle course first wins the prize. You can also award a prize to the team that cheers loudest.

When the obstacle race is finished, ask the students who were blindfolded the following questions:

- Did you feel like the person you were carrying knew where you were supposed to go better than you did?
- Even though you knew he or she could see, was it hard to trust your partner at first? Why or why not?
- Did it get easier or harder as you went farther? Why?
- How did you feel about your partner when you ran into something?

Now ask the winning team why they think they won the race. Transition to the next step by explaining that in this game, each person had to trust his or her guide. That trust allowed them to have faith that the person would lead them the right way. Today, we're going to check out a lesser-known follower of Christ who He said had greater faith in His power than anyone else He had met before.

MESSAGE

Option 1: Trust Me. For this option, you need several Bibles and enough space for students to spread out.

Ask students to spread out so they cannot touch another person to the front, back or side of them. Ask them to hold their arms out to the side (shoulder level) and to close their eyes, keeping them shut. Explain that no matter what you say, they need to keep their eyes closed until you give the okay for them to open them. Tell them that no one will touch them—and that they should trust you about this.

As you continue to explain that they can trust you, begin to walk around between students without touching anyone. Tell them how much you like to tickle people—especially when they aren't expecting it. Remind them to keep their eyes closed, and then talk about how much you also like to give wet willies (putting your wet finger in someone's ear). After a few minutes, let students open their eyes.

Ask the group, "Who opened your eyes—even for a peek?" For those students who confess they did, ask, "Why did you decide that you needed to open your eyes? Did you hear me say that no one would be touched?" (*Most will answer yes.*) Ask, "Was anyone touched?" (*The answer is no.*)

Ask students to close their eyes again, and again promise that they won't be touched. For the next 30 seconds, stay in the front of the room and reassure your students that they can relax and trust that they will not be touched. When 30 seconds are up, ask, "Was everyone able to keep his or her eyes closed? Why were you able to trust me this time?"

Explain that your story today is about someone who trusted 100 percent in Jesus' words. Distribute Bibles as you give background to the story: Jesus was born a Jew in the ancient Middle Eastern region of Judea, which was ruled by foreign Roman soldiers and government officials. Many of Jesus' fellow Jews hated the Romans, and some even wanted to raise an army to kick them out of Judea. Our story today is about one of the soldiers stationed in Judea, in the city of Capernaum. He was a centurion, a commanding officer in the Roman army, with 80 to 100 men under his command. Not only was he a despised foreigner, but also it is likely that he was not a believer in the One God of Israel, who sent His Son to be Israel's Messiah.

Invite five students to read Luke 7:1-10. Have them each read two verses. When they finish, discuss the following:

- How did the centurion decide he could trust Jesus? (*He had heard about Jesus, which probably means he had heard about how Jesus had healed others.*)
- What did he do that demonstrated his trust? (*He sought Jesus to meet his need.*)
- According to the centurion, what did he and Jesus have in common? (*Both had authority over people who served under them.*)
- If both had authority over people, why would the centurion come to Jesus? (*He knew that Jesus had a different and more powerful authority over things that the centurion could not control.*)
- What does Jesus mean by "faith"? (*If students have a hard time answering this, have them read Hebrews 11:1.*)
- Why was the centurion credited with so great a faith? (*His faith was so great because he knew that Jesus didn't even need to be present for Him to heal the servant. He knew that just Jesus' words would do the job.*)
- What was the result of his trust in Jesus? (*His servant was healed. The centurion's faith and the faith of those in his household—and maybe even that of his neighbors—probably grew as well.*)[1]

Option 2: Faith in Authority. For this option, you need several Bibles.

Have those in the group imagine that they were the ruler of the universe and had authority over everything. What is one thing they would do with their power? Allow students to each share *one* thing they would do with their power.

Youth Leader Tip

Challenging students is essential to building their faith. Ask tough questions: "Why do you believe that?" "Where does it say that in the Bible?" Then be prepared with resources to help them find answers.

Continue by stating that today, we're going to look at someone who was a great ruler and had great authority and power. Distribute Bibles as you give background to the story: Jesus was a Jew who lived in the ancient Middle Eastern region of Judea, which at the time was ruled by the Romans. Many of Jesus' fellow countrymen hated the Romans, and a group known as the Zealots even wanted to raise an army to kick them out of Judea. Our story today is about one of these Roman soldiers stationed in the city of Capernaum. He was a centurion in the Roman army and had 80 to 100 men under his command. Not only was he a despised foreigner, but also it is likely that he was not a believer in the One God of Israel, who sent His Son to be Israel's Messiah.

Ask volunteers to read Luke 7:1-10. When each person is finished, discuss the following questions:

- Who was the person in authority in this story? (*Some may say the centurion and some may say Jesus. Affirm either answer and continue.*)
- Why do you think the centurion trusted Jesus so much? (*He had heard about Him; see Luke 7:3.*)
- What do you think the centurion had heard about Jesus? (*He was an amazing teacher; He could heal people; He performed miracles.*)
- What did the centurion do that demonstrated his trust? (*In Luke 7:3,6-7, we read that he sought Jesus to meet his need and then said that Jesus did not need to come to his house but only needed to say the word for his servant to be healed.*)
- According to the centurion, what did he and Jesus have in common? (*Both had authority over people who served under them.*)
- If both had authority, why would the centurion need to come to Jesus? (*He knew that Jesus had more powerful authority over things that the centurion could not control.*)

Ask a volunteer to read Psalm 107:19-20, and then ask the following:

- How does this passage relate to the story of the centurion? (*Both talk about the authority and power of Jesus' words.*)
- What does it mean to have faith? (*If students have a hard time answering this, have them read Hebrews 11:1.*)
- Why was the centurion credited with so great a faith? (*His faith was so great because he knew that Jesus didn't even need to be present for Him to heal the servant. He knew that just Jesus' words would do the job.*)

• What was the result of his trust in Jesus? (*His servant was healed—see Luke 7:10. The centurion's faith and the faith of those in his household—and maybe even that of the neighbors—probably grew as well.*)

DIG

Option 1: Meeting Needs. For this option, you need 3" x 5" index cards and pens or pencils.

Divide students into groups of five or six and distribute one index card and pen or pencil to each student. Explain that we've just read about a man who realized that he couldn't meet the need to heal his servant on his own but needed to look to Jesus. We may not be military rulers, and we may not have servants who are sick, but we do have needs of our own. Instruct students to use the index cards to write down a need they have (clarify that it should be a *real* need). Ask them to place their cards face down in the center of their group and mix them up. Groups should then choose one card at a time from the pile and discuss what would happen if they relied on themselves for that need, and what would happen if they brought that need to Jesus.

Allow a few minutes of discussion, and then collect the cards and randomly choose a few of them, asking the group that had the chosen card to share what they discussed. Ask if there is anything that is so hard that we can't rely on God to work it out. Students will likely say no, at which point you should ask them, "Sure, we say that, but why don't we often bring our needs to Jesus, even if we say we should?" (*We don't really mean it; we can't see Jesus; we're not sure if He will really work it out.*) Ask the group what else we tend to rely on instead of Jesus. (*Friends, parents, good luck, that time will change the situation.*) Ask if it is wrong to rely on other people or things to help us with a problem or need. (*No.*)

Conclude by stating that sometimes Jesus helps us by having others help us, but first we need to ask Him for help with our needs and then listen for His answer, rather than try to take care of it ourselves or rely on others.

Option 2: She Said Yes. For this option, you need a copy of "She Said Yes" (found on the next page), a whiteboard and a dry-erase marker.

Explain that Cassie Bernall was one of the 13 high school students who were shot and killed by two fellow students at Columbine High School in Colorado on April 20, 1999. It seems that when the gunman asked her if she believed in God, either Cassie or her friend said yes. There's no way to know if

She Said Yes

This is what two of Cassie Bernall's friends had to say about her after she was shot and killed by a fellow student at Columbine High School on April 20, 1999.

I wasn't surprised when I heard what happened to her on April 20. That was Cassie. And I think what she did was really admirable—to stand up for what you believe, no matter what. But I never really knew her religious side. Like, she didn't push it on anyone. Okay, one time in class she was reading this little Bible. I asked her what she was doing and she said, "Reading the Bible."

—**Eliza**, a fellow junior at Columbine High School

I can't explain what it was about Cassie—she was just different. She was nice to everyone she talked to at school, and she never judged anyone for how they dressed or looked. I only found out that she was religious and all that after she was killed. We talked about other things, like snowboarding. I told her that I knew how to snowboard, but I couldn't turn very well. She said, "Oh, I'll help you work on it; I'm going snowboarding next week. If you want to come along, give me a call." So we were planning on going snowboarding together. She offered to take me along with her even though she didn't really know me.

—**Kayla**, another classmate at Columbine High School

Cassie was the one who uttered the word, but we do know that she was someone who knew how to rely on Jesus—so much so that others could see the difference in her life.

Read "She Said Yes" to students, and then discuss the following:

- What difference did Cassie's friends notice about her?
- Do you think it's okay that not everyone knew about Cassie's "religious" side?
- Do you think people know about your "religious" side?
- How does your faith in God affect the way you think, feel and act at school?
- Have others ever noticed the difference in you? What did they say?
- If someone were to ask you, "Do you believe in God?" would you be able to answer yes with certainty and conviction?

Explain that while most of us won't ever be in the position where our answer will determine whether or not we die, we do have the chance to say yes to God every day. We say yes every time we come to Him with our needs, even if we're scared (like Cassie must have been) or even just in everyday life. Ask the group to list some everyday situations or worries for junior-highers in which they need to have faith in God and give Him their needs. (*Answers might include what to wear, how to fit in, how to not look stupid, what friends to have, how to relate to the opposite sex, how to respond to peer pressure, how to keep their parents happy, how to maintain their grades, how to stay safe, and so forth.*) List the responses on the whiteboard.

Conclude by asking the group how having faith in God can allow them to handle these situations differently. (*Answers may include knowing that following Him is the right thing to do, that He is there for them, that they can know that they are not alone, experiencing His peace, and so forth.*)

APPLY

Option 1: Pillar of Faith. For this option, you need your Bible, a deck of playing cards (any type), one copy of "Faith Pillar Bookmarks" (found on the next page) for every four students, and pens or pencils. Ahead of time, cut the handouts into individual bookmarks.

Divide students into groups of three or four and give each group five playing cards. Instruct groups to build a small card house, using the first three cards

Faith Pillar Bookmarks

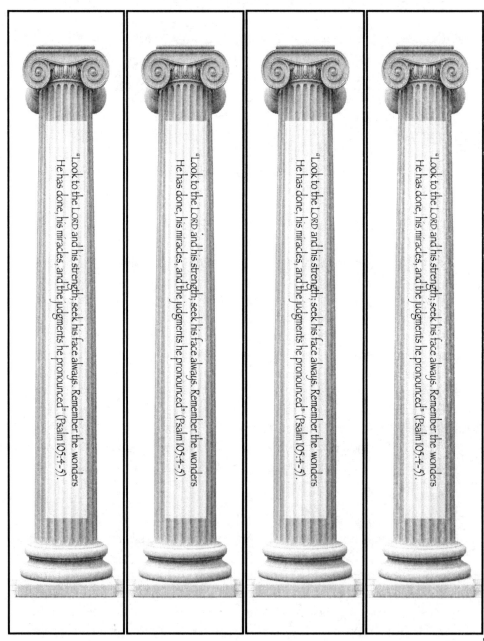

"Look to the LORD and his strength; seek his face always. Remember the wonders He has done, his miracles, and the judgments he pronounced" (Psalm 105:4–5).

"Look to the LORD and his strength; seek his face always. Remember the wonders He has done, his miracles, and the judgments he pronounced" (Psalm 105:4–5).

"Look to the LORD and his strength; seek his face always. Remember the wonders He has done, his miracles, and the judgments he pronounced" (Psalm 105:4–5).

"Look to the LORD and his strength; seek his face always. Remember the wonders He has done, his miracles, and the judgments he pronounced" (Psalm 105:4–5).

to make an *H* and the last two cards placed on top as an A-frame roof. Allow a few moments for building, and then ask which of the cards is the most essential to this structure. (*The middle card of the* H). Explain that one card allows the rest of the cards to stay standing. It is a pillar of strength.

Distribute the bookmarks and pens or pencils, and then ask students to write on their bookmark one or two events or situations in their lives where they had faith in God and saw Him work. Maybe they stood up for what was right in school, or they witnessed their aunt's cancer begin healed, or they had a friend become a Christian, or they went on a missions trip where they really had to depend on God. You can also share a brief example from your own life.

Explain that whatever that faith moment is for them, it represents their faith pillar. A faith pillar can give them strength the next time their life gets tough and they need to trust God. It is something they can remember when they are having a hard time, reminding them of how God was there for them at that time—and how He will always be there in the future.

Suggest that students put their faith pillar bookmarks in their Bible or schoolbooks. Conclude by asking them to remember their faith pillars often and add to them as they see God working in their lives. This will help them experience God's peace as they place their faith in Him.

Option 2: Prayer Reminder. For this option, you need one 6-inch to 8-inch piece of string or rope for every student.

Explain to the group that some of their non-Christian friends may have such big needs that they feel lost and desperate—it's almost as if they were in a pit. Take some time to develop this image by explaining that these friends desperately want out of their miserable situation, but they don't know what to do. Maybe they've even prayed about it, but since God didn't change the situation, they decided that He either doesn't care or that He doesn't exist. They wanted Him to be their rope out of the pit, and He wasn't, so now they're even further away from Him.

Youth Leader Tip

Before presenting an activity or game to your group, test it! Check measurements, evaluate hazards and determine time limits, always keeping your students' abilities and attention spans in mind.

Hold up a piece of string or rope. Explain that although God sometimes erases our needs, as He did with the centurion's servant, He often doesn't take us out of our pit. Instead, He gets right there with us in the middle of the pit. Ask the group how we should feel if we know that He is with us in the pit, even if He chooses not to release us from it. (*We feel joy, peace and love because we know that God is with us even in the midst of the tough stuff.*)

Distribute the strings or rope, and then conclude by stating that this is a prayer reminder. Whenever the students see it, they can remember to pray for one of three needs for their non-Christian friends: (1) that God will take him or her out of the pit of need; (2) that their friend will realize that God is with him or her in the midst of the pit; or (3) that their friend will want to know God more. Note to the group that when God does the latter, sometimes this is how our friends come to know Him as their Savior.

Close in prayer, asking students to pray for one friend who isn't a Christian to get to know Jesus.

REFLECT

The following short devotions are for the students to reflect on and answer during the week. You can make a copy of these pages and distribute to your class or download and print from **www.gospellight.com/uncommon/jh_ the_new_testament.zip.**

1—WHAT DO YOU HOPE FOR?

Don't even think about doing anything else before you flip to Hebrews 11:1.
   What's something you're hoping for in the near future?

- ❑ A gooey, chocolate-chocolate chip sundae
- ❑ An autograph from your favorite musician or sports hero
- ❑ The girl or guy of your dreams to sit next to you in class
- ❑ Your teacher to forget the science test

Hard to choose, isn't it? There's one thing that all four options have in common: They're all temporary—here today and gone tomorrow.
   Hebrews 11:1 gives us something to hope for that won't be gone tomorrow: our faith. It helps us be sure of God's presence and joy in this lifetime and confident of eternal life with Him after we die. Spend a few minutes asking God how you can have more faith and certainty in Him, even if He is invisible.

2—GIVE GOD THE BEST

If you like the biggest piece of pie, turn quickly to Hebrews 11:4.
   It's pie time and your mom hands you the knife. *Bummer,* you think to yourself. You were really hoping that your mom would have given the knife to your younger brother, Christopher. That way he'd have to do the cutting, which meant, according to the family rule, "You-Cut-I-Choose," you'd get to choose the first piece of pie. But now you're stuck.
   We're so quick to want the biggest piece of pie, the most whipped cream, the best slice of pizza. Abel wanted the best meat from the animal, but it wasn't for himself; it was for God. Even though he was murdered by his brother, Cain, his faith still speaks loudly today. He had faith that God would take care of him, so of course he could give God anything and everything that he had.
   How can you give God your best today? If you have faith that He will take care of you, you can give Him every part of your life with no worries.

3—NOT FOR THE FAINT OF HEART

If you're someone who likes adventure movies, race to Hebrews 11:32-40.

Let's say your dad makes you choose to do one of the following. Which would be the worst choice?

- ❑ Cleaning a sewer without gloves
- ❑ Eating liver for dinner 17 days in a row
- ❑ Living in a room with a mouse for a month

None of these options are good, but at least none of them could cost your life! In Hebrews 11:32-40, we learn about all sorts of heroes from the Bible who had to live through *much* worse things—things that could have cost them their lives (and sometimes did). Yet even if they didn't immediately triumph over their immediate circumstances, every single one of them was blessed by God.

Maybe you're not in danger of being sawed in two or put in prison, but you're probably facing some tough things. Take a few minutes today to ask God to help you have the kind of faith that will help you in the midst of the hard stuff you're going through right now.

4—CAN HE REALLY DO ANYTHING?

Quick! Grab your Bible and flip to James 1:5-8.

"I'm a grasshopper. I'm a grasshopper." You're getting a little tired of your little brother wearing all green and hopping around the house, constantly chanting, "I'm a grasshopper. I'm a grasshopper." After a week of this, you finally ask him what he thinks he's doing. He tells you that in his Sunday School class, he read James 1:5-8, so he figures if he has *faith* that God can make him into a grasshopper, God will!

How would you answer your little brother? In one sense, of course, God can do anything, including change a human into a grasshopper. However, God only does things if they fit into *His* will and if they are good for us. As far as we know, there are no recorded instances of human-to-grasshopper conversions.

When you pray, do you *really* believe that God can do anything? Spend a few minutes thinking of all the amazing things God has done (just look outside at His creation and you're bound to get some ideas).

Today and tomorrow, try to remember these awesome things so that you'll be more confident that God can do anything!

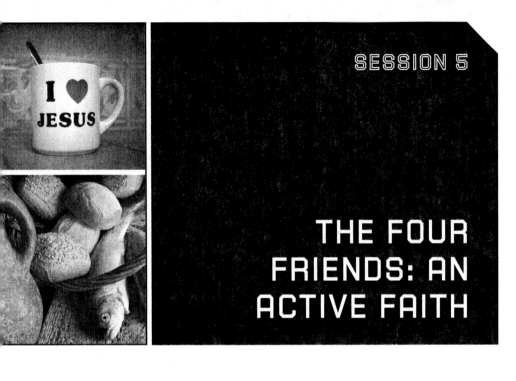

THE FOUR FRIENDS: AN ACTIVE FAITH

THE BIG IDEA

Loving others means looking out for all of their needs, including their spiritual ones.

SESSION AIMS

In this session you will guide students to (1) learn that Jesus offers the best kind of help to hurting people; (2) feel peace when they give their own needs to Jesus; and (3) act by bringing a hurt to Jesus today.

THE BIGGEST VERSE

"When Jesus saw their faith, he said to the paralytic, 'Son, your sins are forgiven'" (Mark 2:5).

OTHER IMPORTANT VERSES

Psalm 139:13; Mark 2:1-12; 14:53-65; Romans 12:9-15; Philippians 4:6-7

Note: Additional options and worksheets in $8^1/_2$" x 11" format for this session are available for download at **www.gospellight.com/uncommon/jh_the_new_testament.zip**.

STARTER

Option 1: Looking Out for Number One. For this option, you need two or three bags of assorted candies and six or seven assorted magazines—beauty, news and sports—for every four to five students.

Greet the students and ask them to sit in groups of four or five. Distribute six or seven magazines to each group and instruct students to find and then tear out advertisements or articles that encourage people to be self-centered, thinking mostly about themselves (for example, "Tight Tummy in Two Weeks," "Learn How to Get the Best Guy/Girl," "Be a Better You"). As groups are busy looking through the ads, begin to distribute the candy, giving out different amounts and kinds, so that it becomes pretty obvious that some groups have more candy (or better candy) than others.

After six to eight minutes, ask each group to pick its top three or four ads/articles and share them with the large group. If you want, you can have the whole group vote on the top three most self-centered ads.

Discuss why magazines would want to use these kinds of advertisements and articles. (*Because they know people are ultimately more concerned with themselves than others.*) Now ask the students to turn this to themselves: *How self-centered are you?* Explain that there's a good way to tell: Have them think about when you were giving candy away and some groups got more than others. What were they thinking or feeling about other people? (*Probably that it wasn't fair that some got better or more candy than they did.*) Ask if any of them thought about giving their candy to someone else.

Explain that while the group was looking for ads and articles that were self-centered, they ended up thinking more about themselves than others. The advertisers are right—we really are self-focused. Today, we're going to learn how to be less self-focused by checking out four followers of Jesus who learned to make others number one.

Option 2: Incredible Injuries. For this option, you need several Bibles, several adult volunteers, items for an obstacle course, envelopes, scissors and one copy of "Incredible Injuries" (found on the next page) for every 10 to 12 students. Cut the copies of "Incredible Injuries" into puzzle pieces, placing each complete set in a separate envelope.

Ahead of time, prepare an obstacle-filled path (chairs to go around, tables to go under, and so forth) using multiple rooms, if possible. Explain the activity to adult volunteers and invite them to use "blackout" and "wake-up" signals to create some drama and fun during the activity. (*Note*: The obstacle course should

INCREDIBLE INJURIES

Hush! You cannot talk for any reason during the game. Your tongue has been ripped out and you are only able to grunt.

Close those peepers! Your eyes have been injured from flying debris and you are blind. Keep them closed and allow yourself to be led from place to place.

Huh? You were too close to the explosion and the sound caused your eardrums to burst. During the game, you can't understand anything anyone says.

The great thinker. You lost the use of your body except your head. You can't sit, stand or move anything but your head. You'll need to be carried around.

One-arm Louie. During the crash one of your arms was broken. You cannot use it at all during the game.

Them's the breaks! A suitcase fell from the overhead bin and crushed your arms. You cannot use either arm throughout the game.

Hop diggity dog! Your left leg is completely useless. You must hop on your right leg or be helped by someone else.

Missing a limb! Flying debris has severed your legs. During the game, you can use only your arms.

Dopey, Sleepy! When you hear the words "blackout," you faint and fall to the ground. Strangely, the words "wake up" restore you to consciousness.

Must've been the lucky rabbit's foot. Fortunately, you have escaped all harm from the crash and are free of injury.

And they say the restroom isn't safe during landing. It seems you have escaped all harm during the crash and are free of injury.

Wipe that sweat from your brow! It was a close call, but you have escaped all harm and are completely free of injury.

not take more than 8 to 12 minutes to complete. Keep the safety of students in mind and remember that some will be carrying others through the course.)

Greet students and divide them into groups of 10 to 12. If there are enough adult volunteers, ask each to supervise a group. Set up the game by stating that each group has just been in a serious plane crash and most of them have been injured. The crash occurred in a remote part of the country where help will not be able to reach them.

Distribute an envelope to each group and explain that each envelope has slips of paper describing different injuries. Each group member is to pull out one slip of paper and read it but not share it with anyone. When the game begins, each student is to act out exactly what his or her injury is (for example, if they are blind, they need to keep their eyes closed; if they have a broken arm, they can't use it). Each group's task is to transport everyone to safety as quickly as it can. No one may be left behind.

Begin the game and end it when most of the groups have finished the obstacle course. Ask students to stay in their groups as they sit down, and then discuss the following questions:

- What was your first thought when the game began? (*Get through the course.*)
- How did your team accomplish the task? (*They worked together and helped each other.*)
- What about those of you who didn't complete the course? What happened? (*They didn't listen to each other; everyone was doing his or her own thing; they didn't help each other.* Note—*Be careful not to allow students to blame one another here!*)
- For those of you who weren't injured as badly, was your first thought about getting yourself through the course or about helping the rest of the team through?
- If you could do this game over again, what would you do differently?

Youth Leader Tip

In youth games, controlled chaos is a good thing. Give clear instructions, set boundaries and have adult supervision in place. In this way, you can give your students the freedom to have fun!

Conclude by stating that this game shows how easy it is for us to be self-centered, putting ourselves first. The problem with this is that putting ourselves first not only hurts others, but eventually we're hurt too because we miss out on the opportunity to help others. Today we're going to check out four followers of Jesus who knew what it means to think of others first.

MESSAGE

Option 1: Four Friends. For this option, you need several Bibles and a copy of "Four Friends: A Melodrama" (found on the next page).

Begin by asking for 13 volunteers to play a part in a fun drama sketch. Explain that whenever you read where an action or statement is called for, the actor playing the part must act it out. Be sure to pause at the appropriate places to allow for the action. The audience's job is to cheer the actors on. After you've finished the melodrama, thank the actors for their award-winning performances and have them rejoin the group. (*Note:* If your group is too small for 13 volunteers, have some students play more than one role; this can actually be pretty hilarious.)

Distribute Bibles, invite students to open them to Mark 2:1-12, and explain that this is the biblical version of the story they just saw in action. Offer this background information: During His earthly ministry, Jesus gained a reputation all over Judea as an amazing healer. All four of the Gospels record miraculous healings, which Jesus said were a sign that the kingdom of God had arrived. Today, we understand the Gospels to be eyewitness accounts of God's kingdom coming in, while the Epistles of the New Testament are letters to the earliest believers about how to live as citizens in the Kingdom. Taken together, the New Testament books tell us modern-day followers of Jesus what He did and how we should respond to Him.

Ask three or four students to take turns reading aloud two or three verses at a time. After they have finished, discuss the following:

- What was the paralytic man's need? (*He was paralyzed.*)
- Why did Jesus tell him that his sins were forgiven? (*Because that was his real need. He had physical needs, but the greater need was forgiveness through Jesus.*)[1]
- If Jesus had only healed his physical problem and the paralytic left, would his needs have been met? (*Physically, yes, but his biggest need wouldn't have been met. Spiritually, he needed Jesus most of all.*)

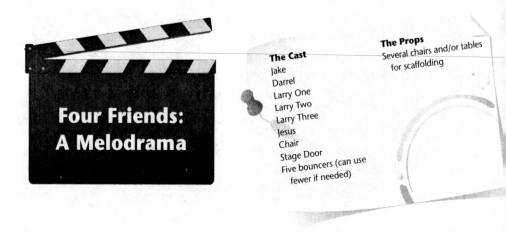

The Cast
Jake
Darrel
Larry One
Larry Two
Larry Three
Jesus
Chair
Stage Door
Five bouncers (can use fewer if needed)

The Props
Several chairs and/or tables for scaffolding

Four Friends: A Melodrama

There once was a guy named Jake. Jake was a regular guy—except that he was paralyzed from the neck down. Jake had four great friends, Larry, Larry, Larry and Darrel. (Yes, three of them were named Larry.) One day Darrel was sitting on a chair, reading the newspaper. When he saw an article that mentioned that Jesus was going to be in town that weekend, he whispered to himself, "Jesus is going to be in town this weekend! I'm going to get tickets. We need to take Jake to see Him."

He immediately called to reserve tickets, but he was too late. He was sad—so sad that he pushed his chair aside and sat on the floor. Jesus was already sold out! At this point, Darrel began to cry and even wail. "What am I going to do?" he said. "I'll call Larry, Larry and Larry; maybe they'll have an idea."

Larry, Larry and Larry came over to see Darrel. When they got there, he was still sobbing and blowing his nose. "What's wrong?" said Larry. Sitting in the middle of the floor sobbing and blowing his nose, Darrel said, "Jesus is in town and I want us to take Jake, but the tickets are already sold out. What are we going to do?" And he sobbed and blew his nose some more.

The four men sat and thought about it for a while. Suddenly, all three Larrys had an idea. "I've got an idea!" they yelled. Then they argued about who was going to talk first. A fight almost broke out when Darrel stepped in and said, "Hey, let's not fight; we're trying to help out Jake." Pointing to one of the Larrys, he said, "You go first." Larry (One) said, "Well, I say we sneak him in." The other Larrys yelled, "That was my idea!" So they all agreed and planned a way to get Jake backstage.

Later that night they picked up Jake and took him to the amphitheater where Jesus was. They knocked on the stage door, but no one answered. They decided to try the stage door to see if it was open; it was, so they sneaked in and found five bouncing bouncers blocking the way to Jesus. They decided to take Jake up on the scaffolding above Jesus and lower him down. So they climbed up and up and up and up and then dropped Jake. He landed right in front of Jesus. When Jesus saw Jake, He said, "I forgive you of your sins; now get up and go home." The audience was amazed and Jake busted out with a few dance moves as he left the stage.

— The End —

- All of us have physical needs and spiritual needs. Both are important, but which is greater? (*Our spiritual need for Jesus.*)
- What if Jesus hadn't healed the man's physical body but had forgiven him? Would his needs have been met? (*His true need was met. He will spend eternity with Jesus. Jesus showed compassion and healed him, but the physical healing wasn't necessary for him to follow Jesus.*)
- What role did his friends play in helping the paralyzed man? (*They recognized his need and helped him. They not only saw his need to be healed but also saw the big picture—his need for spiritual healing through Jesus.*)[2]

Option 2: Make the Call. For this option, you need your Bible, a working phone, a clear pitcher of water and a stick long enough to stick out of the top of the pitcher. Ahead of time, get the phone number of your local mayor, state or federal senator, or maybe even the White House. (*Optional:* Arrange ahead of time to call an adult volunteer—pretending that you're calling the VIP's office—who will answer the phone and inform you that the VIP is busy.)

Begin by sharing about a friend of yours who has a pretty serious need, such as a new job or a better relationship with his or her parents. Ask students if they know anyone who has a need, and then invite them to share about that need without giving the person's name or any specific details that will make the person's identity too obvious. Continue by explaining that when we have needs, there are at least two reasons that Jesus is the place to turn.

The first reason is because *Jesus is never too busy for us.* Ask, "Don't you hate it when you have a big need and you go to someone for help, only to find that they're too busy for you?" Explain that you have a question that you would like to talk over with the mayor/senator/president (whomever you have chosen). Use the phone to try to call the person. Of course, you won't get through to him or her—especially if it's the weekend or evening. (*Note:* If there's even the slightest chance that you will get through to the person, call ahead and let the person answering the phone know that you will be calling back later, and when you do, he or she should tell you that the person you're asking for is too busy to be bothered right now. Your students will be shocked, and probably pretty impressed, that you had the guts to even make the call!)

Continue by stating that there is Someone who is *never* too busy for us. Read Mark 2:1-5 and explain that even in the midst of a crowd, when Jesus saw the friends and the paralytic, He stopped what He was doing to help them.

The second reason we can turn to Jesus when we have needs is that *He knows what is best for us.* Read Mark 2:5 one more time, and then ask the group why Jesus forgave the man's sins when it was obvious that he was paralyzed. (*The answer is that anyone could see the man's physical need, but Jesus knows what he really needed, even if the man and those around him did not.*) Put the stick into the pitcher of water and point out the distortion of the part of the stick that's in the water. Ask the group to imagine that the stick is their lives and they see only the part where the water distorts the stick. Only God can see beyond the illusion and see what they really need.

Read Mark 2:6-12, and then conclude by stating that Jesus knew the paralytic's real need was for forgiveness of his sins. However, because Jesus cared about the man's physical needs, He healed his paralysis *and* forgave him for his sins. Now that's something to celebrate!

DIG

Option 1: Which Would You Choose? For this option, you need a copy of "Which Would You Choose?" (found on the next page) for each student, and pens or pencils.

Divide students into groups of two or three and distribute "Which Would You Choose?" and pens or pencils. Instruct students to mark their choices and then discuss them in their groups. Allow a few minutes for groups to discuss, and then explain that you have one more choice to give them that's a little more serious: *Would they choose being penniless, in poor health and knowing Jesus, or being rich, in great health and not knowing Jesus? Why?* Allow a few responses from the group.

Continue by discussing the following questions:

- Our society has a lot of prescriptions for feeling better. What are some things people do to feel better or escape their own pain? (*Drugs, alcohol, relationships, pornography, shopping, working out, eating, smoking, sex, violence, and so forth.*)
- What is wrong with turning to these things? (*They only work for a while. The fun or excitement wears off.*)
- Can we solve people's problems by ourselves? (*Not usually; some of them are way too big for us.*)
- Could the four friends solve the paralyzed man's problem? (*No—they took him to Jesus.*)
- How can we help others who need to know Jesus? (*Pray for them, talk to them about Him, invite them to youth group and to church.*)

Which Would You Choose?

❏ Being told by a friend that you have bad breath	OR	❏ Being told that the girl or guy that you like doesn't like you
❏ Listening to country-western music for a month	OR	❏ Listening to opera music for the next month
❏ Wearing the same clothes to school every day for a month	OR	❏ Going to school without a shower for a month
❏ Reading two hours of English literature after school	OR	❏ Doing two hours of vacuuming and dusting
❏ Driving a car (yes, yourself!)	OR	❏ Driving a motorcycle
❏ Killing a spider with your hands	OR	❏ Killing a snail with your bare feet
❏ Going a month without using a phone or texting	OR	❏ Going a month without watching television
❏ For the girls: Going a week without makeup	OR	❏ Going a week without your favorite pair of shoes
❏ For the guys: Going a week without any sugar	OR	❏ Going a week without playing or watching sports
❏ Breaking your leg	OR	❏ Breaking the arm you write with

Conclude by stating that our hardships in life now are temporary—as hard as that is to believe sometimes. But having Jesus in our lives is eternal. When our lives end on earth, we will live forever with Jesus.

Option 2: Big Problems. For this option, you need copies of "Big Problems" (found on the next page) and pens or pencils. Divide the students into small groups of 6 to 8 each and assign a case study from the handout to each group. Ask the four groups to discuss the following two questions about the teen in their case study:

- What are his or her needs?
- If you were a close friend, how could you help him or her?

Allow five to seven minutes for groups to discuss the questions, and then ask each of the small groups to share their ideas. Once they have done so, point out that all of the teens in these case studies have huge needs. Although close friends could help them a little bit, they probably couldn't bring Jan's parents back together, bring Steve's sister or his leg back, get Dave's dad to stay sober, or help Sarah know how much her parents care about her.

Conclude by stating that when we encounter people's problems that are too big for us to handle, the story of the four friends and the paralyzed man can help us know what to do. We can help by comforting and supporting our friend in their time of need. Most importantly, we can point our friends to Jesus by praying for them and talking to them about Him or inviting them to youth group and church.

APPLY

Option 1: Unload Your Rocks. For this option, you need your Bible, a back-pack, several rocks, a cross (preferably one with a base for standing it up), copies of "Rock Cutout" (see the following page—this should ideally be copied on brown or gray paper), some worship music (provided by either a recording or a worship team), and pens or pencils. Set up the cross in your meeting place where you'll be able to put rocks around the base and cut out the paper rocks.

Select a volunteer to come forward, and ask him or her to put on the empty backpack. Ask students to name some common needs, hurts and concerns that junior-highers have today. For each one named, put a real rock in the backpack.

Choose one of the following four case studies to read with your group, and then discuss the following questions:

1. What are the person's needs?
2. If you were a close friend, how could you help him or her?

CASE STUDY 1

Jan's parents separated last week. They had been fighting a lot lately and it seems that they've just given up trying to get along. Jan is feeling like it's her fault that her parents are separated and she's feeling depressed and alone.

CASE STUDY 2

Steve woke up in the hospital. He asked what had happened. The doctor told him that he had been in an accident. A drunk driver hit his car as he was driving home from the football game with his younger sister. The doctor told him that in the accident Steve's right leg was crushed and it had to be amputated. Then the doctor broke the news to him that his sister had been killed in the accident.

CASE STUDY 3

Dave is the class clown. He is always laughing and making jokes. He loves to pull pranks on people—only for fun though; he never wants to hurt anyone. Dave lives with his dad, but he tries not to go home until his dad is asleep because he doesn't want to get caught in one of his drunken rages. He usually hangs out with friends or at the mini-mart until he thinks it's safe to go home.

CASE STUDY 4

Sarah is a straight-A student. She works really hard at making perfect grades. She never seems satisfied with her work and she's always complaining that she probably failed. She feels like her parents think she's a failure because she's not as smart as her older brother. All she wants is for her parents to be happy with her and love her. She's sure that if she just tries hard enough, they will approve of her.

ROCK CUTOUT

As the backpack begins to fill with rocks, explain that all of these things are a heavy burden for anyone to carry. Read Philippians 4:6-7 aloud, and state that when we give our needs to God, it's like taking a stone out of the backpack. Start taking stones out of the backpack and putting them at the base of the cross.

Distribute the paper rocks and a pen or pencil and invite students to give their burdens to God. Instruct them to write down their worries, concerns, hurts and pain on the paper rocks. Play the worship music. When they are done writing, invite them to prayerfully give these things to God as they lay their rocks at the cross. Close your time in prayer, thanking God that we can pray about anything and know His peace.

Option 2: Teardrops. For this option, you need copies of "Teardrop Cutout" (found on the next page), pens or pencils and some courageous students. Cut out the paper teardrops ahead of time.

Begin by explaining that when people come to us in need, it gives us a great chance to help them see that Jesus is the only One who can meet their real needs. Read the following scenario:

Your friend Krista comes to you because she's sick and tired of her step-mom, Lynetta. Lynetta has two of her own kids, Heather and Mark, who have moved in with Krista and her dad. Not only are they little brats, but Lynetta totally favors them, taking them out for special ice cream dates and leaving Krista sitting home alone. Yet she is expected to babysit them at anytime, even when she has other plans. Krista is frustrated with Lynetta and her kids, but even more than that, she's angry with her dad for letting it happen. Krista looks at you and asks what you think she should do. You say . . .

Give students a few minutes to brainstorm, instructing them to focus on things that could help Krista know more about Jesus. Answers might include

Youth Leader Tip
Remember that your job is not to tell students what to believe but to present God's Word, ask questions and provide opportunities for them to apply their faith. Enable students to take ownership of their faith and live it out daily.

Teardrop Cutout

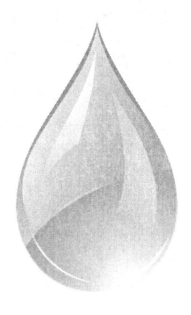
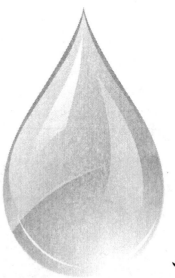

telling Krista, "I'll pray for you" or "I know you're hurting right now and there actually is a perfect dad—He's perfect and He loves you" or "This is a pretty tough thing—how about if I pray for you right now?"

Distribute the paper teardrops and pens or pencils. Explain that the teardrops represent a person in their life who is in need right now. Ask students to write that person's need (no names) on their teardrops. Have them find a partner and discuss both of their friends' needs, brainstorming together how they could be like the four friends and point their friends in need to Jesus. After a few minutes, ask each partner to exchange teardrops so that they can pray for each other's person in need during the coming week.

REFLECT

The following short devotions are for the students to reflect on and answer during the week. You can make a copy of these pages and distribute to your class or download and print from **www.gospellight.com/uncommon/jh_the_new_testament.zip**.

1—DON'T SPEND IT ALL IN ONE PLACE

If you like money, jam over to Acts 2:44-47.

Juanita decided to accept her senior pastor's challenge. He was asking everyone, from little kids to senior citizens, to keep track of all the money they spend during the next month. The goal was for people to understand some of the bizarre—and even frivolous—ways that they spend their money and to prompt them to use their money for different things.

By day six, Juanita knew she was in trouble. She had already spent three times as much money on fruit smoothies as she had on anything else. This continued throughout the whole month; and by the time she had calculated all of her expenses, she realized that with the exception of a new video game she had bought for herself, and of course that new necklace, most of her money went to fruit smoothies.

If Juanita were part of the community of people in Acts 2:44-47, she'd probably be making some different choices. She'd be giving more to others instead of spending it on drinks that were good and nutritious but not essential for her health and survival. If you include the amount of sodas, too, the money she spent on drinks in one month could feed a hungry person for two months.

What about you? Are you spending your money in ways that really count, or are you letting it trickle away on smoothies and gum? Ask God to show you how to spend your money to help others today.

2—HELP IS ON THE WAY

Race on over to Matthew 6:5-8.

Which of the following needs would be the toughest for you to meet if a friend came to you and asked for your help?

- ❑ A loan of $500 to pay the rent, so her family wouldn't be evicted
- ❑ Mechanical help with fixing her family's old minivan that keeps breaking down

❑ Advice to help her and her sister to decide which parent to live with after the divorce

❑ An idea for getting along better with her grandmother

Maybe all of the needs seem pretty tough to you. The reality is that they are all pretty tough. It's so good to know that Matthew 6:5-8 is true—that our Father knows what we need even before we ask. We can go to Him at any time and He'll welcome and understand us.

Think about a need that you have and a need that one of your friends has. Pray about both of those needs, asking God to show you what to do in your own life, as well as how to help your friend.

3—WHAT CAN YOU DO?

If you like TV, flip the channel over to James 2:14-17.

Kyra was flipping the channels, trying to find something to watch after her favorite afternoon cartoon ended. She started channel surfing again during one of its commercial breaks and ended up on a local news channel where some video footage caught her eye. The news story was about some teenagers near Kyra's age who were homeless. Because it was the winter, they nearly froze to death at night. Here Kyra was, watching TV in a warm and cozy family room while people her own age were almost freezing to death.

Kyra decided to do something about it. She went around to all her neighbors, asking them for any old blankets to donate to homeless teens. By calling the TV station, she talked with the reporter who had done the interview and found out where the homeless teens hung out during the day. With her mom and stepbrother, she went down to where they were and handed out the blankets she had collected. That night, although it was still cold outside, there were some homeless teens who were very grateful for Kyra's compassion for them.

Reread James 2:14-17. The next time you hear about someone in need, maybe there will be something you can do to help them. Even if you don't know them, God might be able to work through you!

DAY 4—THE GIRL IN THE HALL

Run, don't walk, over to 1 John 3:16-18.

That new girl in school with the funny shoes is coming toward you. Phew! She stopped at her locker. Just as you turn away, she opens her locker and someone runs past her, knocking her down. Her books and her lunch go flying and everyone around her starts laughing. What is your first reaction?

- ❏ Call her names and tell her how stupid she is
- ❏ Join in with those who are laughing at and mocking her
- ❏ Help her pick up her stuff
- ❏ Drop your own books to cause a diversion, giving her time to pick up her things

If you want to take 1 John 3:16-18 literally, there are two alternatives: You can either help her or drop your own books to divert attention. (The best choice of the two is to help her pick up her things.) Loving in actions means acting. It's not just talking about loving, but letting your hands be the messengers.

Today, make a commitment to help at least one person. That person will feel better, and you probably will too because you are doing the right thing and you will know it.

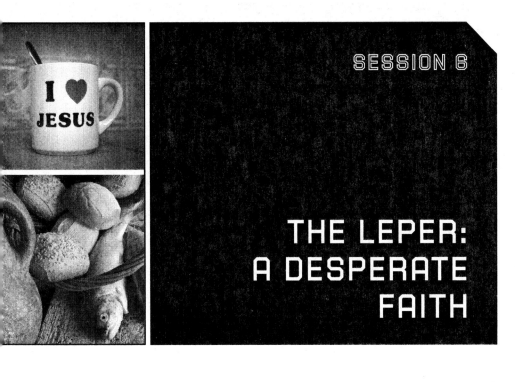

THE LEPER: A DESPERATE FAITH

THE BIG IDEA

Just because we have been forgiven by Jesus doesn't make us perfect or sinless.

SESSION AIMS

In this session you will guide students to (1) recognize that Jesus is the one who forgives them; (2) feel the freedom to admit their faults; and (3) let others see Jesus in the midst of all of their struggles and imperfections.

THE BIGGEST VERSE

"Jesus sent him away at once with a strong warning: 'See that you don't tell this to anyone . . .' Instead he went out and began to talk freely, spreading the news. As a result, Jesus could no longer enter a town openly but stayed outside in lonely places. Yet the people still came to him from everywhere" (Mark 1:43-45).

OTHER IMPORTANT VERSES

Mark 1:40-45; John 10:10; Romans 7:15,24-25; 1 Corinthians 10:13

Note: Additional options and worksheets in 8¹/₂" x 11" format for this session are available for download at **www.gospellight.com/uncommon/jh_the_new_testament.zip**.

STARTER

Option 1: Broken Toys. For this option, you need a warped Frisbee and a jump rope that's too short (at a length that makes it difficult, but not necessarily impossible, to get one or two interesting jumps out of it). You may choose to use other broken items if you have them available, such as a broken skateboard or yo-yo. Ahead of time, hide the Frisbee and jump rope until it's time for the volunteers to use them. (*Note:* You might want to consider doing this option outside or in a large indoor space to make sure no one gets clocked by an out-of-control Frisbee.)

Welcome students and begin the session by explaining that today you're going to give them a chance to set some world records—or at least some youth group ones! Ask for volunteers to see who can throw a Frisbee the farthest and who can jump rope the most times in a row. Ask the volunteers how far they think they can throw the Frisbee and how many times they think they can jump rope. Choose the student who thinks he or she can throw the Frisbee the farthest and the student who thinks he or she can jump rope the longest.

Mark the distance the Frisbee volunteer thinks she can throw; then hand her the warped Frisbee. (You should have an interesting response to the less-than-perfect object and you can apologize for the shape of the Frisbee, looking as surprised as the volunteer.) Ask the volunteer to try to throw the Frisbee as far as she estimated, even though it's warped . . . and suggest to the other students that standing back might be a good idea. Allow for a few attempts and then move on to the jump rope volunteer.

Ask the rope jumper to tell you again how long he thinks he will be able to jump rope. Bring out the rope and when it becomes obvious to the volunteer that the rope is too short, encourage him to try anyway. (After all, a good rope jumper should be able to handle a short rope!) Allow for a couple of attempts; then apologize once more to both volunteers for all the difficulty and invite them to take their seats in the group.

When you are finished, discuss the following:

- What made it difficult to achieve the goals with the Frisbee and the jump rope? (*Both of the items were broken and didn't work right.*)
- What could we have done so that the Frisbee and jump rope worked better? (*Try to reshape the Frisbee, add new rope to the jump rope or get new items.*)
- Before we are able to fix something, what do we need to do? (*Recognize what's wrong with it.*)

- When there are things in our life that don't work or are broken or hurt, what do we need to do before those things can be fixed or healed? (*Recognize the problem.*)

Transition by stating that our lives need to be fixed and we need to be healed. Sometimes we need to be healed physically, but we're going to look at how our hearts need to be healed and forgiven from something that hurts all of us: sin. Today we're going to check out a lesser-known follower of Christ who will help us to understand that just because we're forgiven by Jesus doesn't mean that our lives will be perfect or that we are free from sin.

Option 2: I Need a Medic. For this option, you need several adult volunteers, a box of large rubber bands or several pieces of rope that can be used to tie two people's legs together (three-legged-race style), masking tape and candy or other goodies for prizes. Use masking tape to designate a corner of the room as a hospital.

Greet students and ask for 10 volunteers. Divide the volunteers into two teams and introduce the game by explaining the rules: One team will be "It" and the other team will be "Medics." Those who are It will try to tag all the other students in the room. When students are tagged they will freeze where they are and wave their hands in the air and yell, "I need a Medic!"

The team of Medics will have the job of rescuing everyone who's frozen by touching them and sending them to the hospital, where they will be treated by the adult volunteers by being paired with another victim and having their legs tied together with the rubber bands or rope (three-legged-race style). Once paired up and tied together, they will be released from the hospital to resume the game. If a three-legged team is tagged, the pair automatically becomes It instead of freezing. Play until only a few students are left, and then award the prizes and invite students to take their seats.

After the game, discuss the following:

- Have any of you ever had to be taken to the emergency room? (*You'll probably have quite a few stories to choose from!*)
- What was the first thing they did when you went in? (*They assessed your physical problem to determine how urgent it was.*)
- When there are things in our lives that don't work or are broken or hurt, what do we need to do before those things can be fixed or healed? (*Recognize them.*)

Transition by stating that our lives do need to be fixed and we need to be healed. Sometimes we need to be healed physically, but we're going to look at how our hearts need to be healed from something that hurts all of us: sin. Today we're going to check out a lesser-known follower of Christ who will help us to understand that just because we're healed doesn't mean that our lives will be perfect or that we are free from sin.

MESSAGE

Option 1: Diagnosis: Sin. For this option, you need one envelope and one copy of "Diagnosis: Sin" (found on the next page) for every three to four students, and candy or other goodies for prizes. Copy the worksheet onto card stock. Cut the handouts apart to create several puzzles and place each complete puzzle into an envelope, and then seal the envelopes.

Divide students into groups of three or four and distribute the puzzle envelopes. Explain that when you give the signal, groups are to open their envelopes and assemble their puzzles. Ready? Set. Go! The first team to complete their puzzle wins a prize. Reward the winning team and ask the group what this puzzle was a picture of. (*A medicine bottle.*) Ask what the medicine is a cure for. (*Our sins.*) Then ask for two volunteers to read the Scripture on the puzzle and discuss the following:

- What was wrong with the man in the story? (*He had leprosy.*)[1]
- Knowing his need, what did he decide to do? (*He came to Jesus, got down on his knees and said that he knew that if Jesus was willing, He could heal his leprosy.*)
- What was Jesus' response? (*He willed the leper to be healed.*)
- What did it take for the man with leprosy—an incurable disease—to be healed? (*Asking Jesus to heal him.*)
- How is the illness of sin different than that of the man in the story? (*His illness was physical; sin is an illness in our hearts that causes emptiness, hurt, bitterness, loneliness and many other side effects.*)
- How are these side effects similar to the man's leprosy? (*They seem incurable, they eat away at us and they can be contagious.*)
- What will it take for us to get better? (*Asking Jesus to forgive us of our sin.*)
- Do you think Jesus is willing to heal you of your sin? (*Yes!*)
- Why do you think we still struggle with sins even after we ask Jesus to forgive us of our sins and take over our lives? (*When we ask Jesus to take*

DIAGNOSIS: SIN

A man with leprosy came to Him and begged Him on his knees, "If you are willing, you can make me clean."

Filled with compassion, Jesus reached out His hand and touched the man. "I am willing," He said. "Be clean!" Immediately the leprosy left him and he was cured.

Jesus sent him away at once with a strong warning: "See that you don't tell this to anyone. But go, show yourself to the priest and offer the sacrifices that Moses commanded for your cleansing, as a testimony to them." Instead he went out and began to talk freely, spreading the news. As a result, Jesus could no longer enter a town openly but stayed outside in lonely places. Yet the people still came to him from everywhere (Mark 1:40-45).

over our lives and be our Savior, our healing and forgiveness are once and for all in that the sin that would ultimately keep us from having relationship with God is eliminated. However, we have a subsequent and ongoing need for forgiveness as we learn to turn every area of our lives over to Him, and we still suffer from consequences of that sin in our day-to-day decisions and actions that are disobedient to Him.)

- In Mark 1:40-45, can you see an example of sin, even after a healing? (*Absolutely. The leper, right after his healing, disobeyed Jesus and told lots of people about what had happened, even when Jesus sternly warned him not to.*)

Option 2: Spiritual Health Checklist. For this option, you need several Bibles, copies of "Spiritual Health Checklist" (found on the next page) and pens or pencils. Distribute "Spiritual Health Checklist" and pens or pencils. Ask the group to imagine the following illustration:

You've just entered the ultimate doctor's office—God's—and He wants you to fill out this form of your spiritual health history. Look it over and check off any of the diseases or injuries you think you may have. Don't be afraid to be honest—we've all had a lot of these listed here. I won't ask anyone to share who doesn't volunteer first.

Allow students several minutes to complete the handouts, and then discuss what some of the most common diseases might be. Ask if anyone is willing to share what one of his or hers was (be prepared to lead the way by sharing some of yours).

Continue by stating that right now, we're going to read about someone who had a contagious and eventually fatal disease that—like many on this checklist—seemed incurable. Have students find Mark 1:40-45 in their Bibles. Ask a volunteer to read the passage out loud, and then discuss the following:

- What disease did this man have? (*Leprosy.*)
- What is leprosy? (*A contagious, incurable and deadly disease that affects people's ability to feel their skin. Because they can't feel, they hurt themselves and have terrible sores.*)
- Knowing he had an incurable, contagious, deadly disease, what did this man decide to do? (*He came to Jesus, got down on his knees and said that he knew that if Jesus were willing, He could heal his leprosy.*)

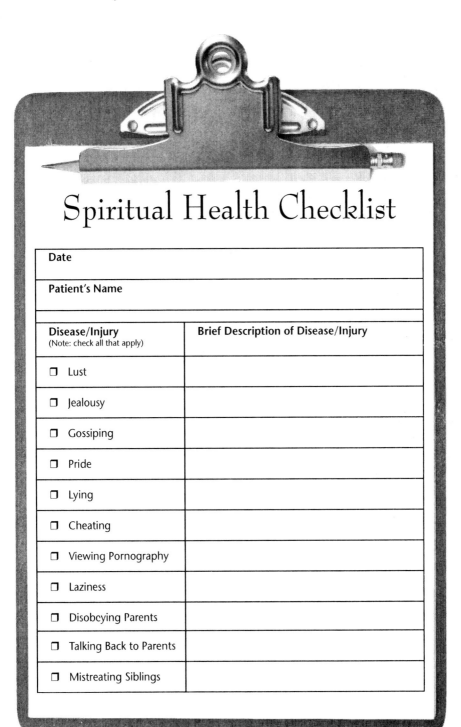

Spiritual Health Checklist

Date	
Patient's Name	
Disease/Injury (Note: check all that apply)	**Brief Description of Disease/Injury**
☐ Lust	
☐ Jealousy	
☐ Gossiping	
☐ Pride	
☐ Lying	
☐ Cheating	
☐ Viewing Pornography	
☐ Laziness	
☐ Disobeying Parents	
☐ Talking Back to Parents	
☐ Mistreating Siblings	

- Why did the man ask Jesus to heal him if He were "willing"? (*Probably because he knew Jesus had the power to heal; so the question was not whether Jesus could heal him, but whether Jesus would heal him.*)
- What was Jesus' response? (*He willed the leper to be healed.*)
- Jesus did something else very unusual in this situation. Can you find it in verse 41? (*He touched the leper, something that no one else would do for fear of catching the contagious disease.*)
- How are the illnesses on our charts different from the illness of the man in the story? (*His was physical; ours are in our hearts and lives.*)
- How are these sins similar to the man's leprosy? (*They both seem incurable, they eat away at us and they can even be contagious.*)
- What will it take for us to be healed? (*Asking Jesus to forgive us.*)
- Do you think Jesus is willing to forgive you? (*Yes!*)
- Why do you think we still struggle with sins even after we ask Jesus to forgive us of our sins and take over our lives? (*When we ask Jesus to take over our lives and be our Savior, our healing and forgiveness are once and for all in that the sin that would ultimately keep us from having relationship with God is eliminated. However, we have a subsequent and ongoing need for forgiveness as we learn to turn every area of our lives over to Him, and we still suffer from consequences of that sin in our day-to-day decisions and actions that are disobedient to Him.*)
- In Mark 1:40-45, can you see an example of sin, even after a healing? (*Absolutely. The leper, right after his healing, disobeyed Jesus and told lots of people about what had happened, even when Jesus sternly warned him not to.*)

DIG

Option 1: Step into the Light. For this option, you need two or three mature student volunteers, a video recorder and a way to play your movie. (*Note:* If there's no such animal as a mature student in your group, you can opt for recruiting high school or adult volunteers for the video interview.)

Ahead of time, create a brief video, filming each volunteer talking about the sins he or she struggles with (being as transparent as possible yet still being appropriate for a 13-year-old audience). Backlight the silhouette of the interview subjects so that their identities can't be seen in the video. End the segment by asking each person to "step into the light," reveal their identities, and talk about how they are letting Jesus heal them from their sin.

Explain to students that you will be showing a serious video—one in which the people are being very vulnerable and sharing real struggles in their lives. After viewing the mini-movie, discuss the following:

- Does being a Christian make a person perfect? (*No.*)
- Do people expect Christians to be perfect? (*Sometimes.*)
- What did the people in the video share with us today? (*They talked about the sin in their lives and the real struggles they face.*)
- What were some of the sins they mentioned? Chances are that at least one of those struggles is something you struggle with too. Do your non-Christian friends know that you struggle with sin? (*Some will say yes, others no.*)
- In order to share Jesus with other people, they need to see our need for Jesus and for His ongoing forgiveness today. Why do you think it's important? (*When they see us being real and that Jesus can change us, they are more likely to believe that Jesus can help them too.*)
- The people in the video didn't stay hidden. They came out of the darkness into the light where their realness was exposed. What are some ways we can be real about our struggles and our need for Jesus' forgiveness? (*Don't pretend to be perfect; share with our friends about what temptations are difficult for us; tell our friends things we did wrong and that we really don't want to behave that way; discuss with them that we have asked Jesus to forgive us and that He continues to work on us, even when we mess up.*)

Option 2: Nobody's Perfect. For this option, you need just a really good book—this one! Share the following case study:

Casey has grown up in church her whole life and enjoys going. She loves her family and it shows. In fact most people, both at church and at school, often comment on how wonderful her family is—sometimes they tease that they are the Brady Bunch, or the Cleaver Family from the old black-and-white TV show *Leave It to Beaver*. Casey's teachers and classmates often comment on her bright smile and upbeat personality. She does well in school, earning straight *A*s, and is very athletic. Now that she is in junior high, some of the guys are also starting to notice Casey. Other girls often look at Casey and wish they could be as perfect as she is.

Nicole is one of Casey's good friends. They love to hang out at school, giggle about boys and swap clothes. As much as they hang out, Nicole has never gone to church. No one in her family has. Casey has invited her a few times, but Nicole is never able to come. Let's take a look inside of Nicole's mind:

Casey has it all: a perfect family, no struggles, she never swears, she's always smiling—I wish I could be perfect like her. She doesn't have any problems. I could never go to her church; I could never be that perfect. The moment I walked in the door everybody would stare and ask, "Why is she here? She sure doesn't belong in this place!" Chances are I would really mess it up and say lots of bad words or do bad things. I really like Casey, but I don't think I could ever go to church with her.

Discuss the following:

- Do you think Nicole is right about church? (*Not necessarily; however, many people feel that way about going to church, maybe because of their own insecurities and perceptions, or possibly because we as Christians can create that atmosphere by pretending to be perfect and by being judgmental.*)
- Do you really think Casey is perfect? (*No, nobody is perfect. We all have sin and struggles.*)
- What might be some of Casey's struggles? (*The next part will help answer this. You don't need to give students answers at this point.*)

Continue by stating that you will now take a look inside Casey's mind:

I am really struggling and I don't feel like anyone cares. My parents don't seem to notice me or acknowledge what I've done. That really hurts. I am also having a really hard time not gossiping. I really enjoy spending time with Nicole and my other girlfriends, but it seems like I keep talking about other people. I also really like Brian, but he never notices me—he always talks about Katie. She is so pretty; I wish I could be as pretty as she is. I know people think I'm always happy, but I feel so sad and lonely a lot of the time. God, I know You hear me; thank You for forgiving me when I mess up and for loving me anyway. I hope no one finds out all these bad things in my life—I don't want to let You down.

Conclude by discussing the following:

- Was Nicole right about Casey? (*No, this often happens. We assume that other people never feel like we do or experience the struggles we do.*)
- What are some of Casey's struggles? (*Gaining other people's approval, not feeling important, gossiping, jealousy, sadness, loneliness, not being understood.*)
- How could Casey change her approach in reaching her friend Nicole? (*Being honest and real about her struggles so that Nicole knows that Casey needs healing but has learned to look to Jesus for it.*)
- What are some ways we can be real about our struggles and our need for Jesus' help? (*Don't pretend to be perfect, share with our friends about what temptations are difficult for us, tell our friends about things we've done wrong and that we really don't want to behave that way. Discuss with them how you have asked Jesus to forgive you and that He continues to work on you, even when you mess up.*)

APPLY

Option 1: Bring Him Up. For this option, you need a little of this and a little of that—and this gggggreat book!

Explain to the group that so far we've been talking about recognizing our need to be forgiven and being real, but now it is time to begin sharing our discovery with others. Why is it so hard for us to talk to our friends about Jesus? (*We get embarrassed; we think they won't understand; we worry that they will think we are weird; we think we sound funny or silly when we talk about Jesus; we don't want to be rejected.*)

Continue by asking the group to think about close friends and family who don't know Jesus. They have a problem—sin—that's deadly and eats away at their hearts, but you know Someone who can help them. Don't you want to tell

Youth Leader Tip

As youth leaders, we need to practice what we preach. Never stop examining your heart, admitting your sin and asking Jesus to forgive you. Lead by example and live out your faith.

those friends and family members? Probably, but sometimes it's hard to figure out how to tell them. One way to start is by bringing Jesus up in conversation.

Point out that if students are spending time with Jesus and coming to the youth group and church services, there are plenty of opportunities to bring Him into their conversations. Let them know that you are going to help them to practice bringing Jesus into a conversation with a non-Christian by doing some role-playing. Ask for a volunteer to be the Christian. You will play the part of the non-Christian.

Explain to the volunteer that you're going to have a normal conversation, the kind he or she would have with a friend at lunch, and he or she is going to try to creatively show you how he or she relies on Jesus every day. Give the audience a role, too, by telling the students that at any time, someone from the audience can yell "Freeze!" and you and the volunteer must freeze wherever they are. Someone from the audience can take that opportunity to switch places with either actor, and the role-play will continue.

Begin by talking with the volunteer about a great movie you saw this weekend, and allow students to dive in any time they want. Allow the role-play to go on for several minutes, and then discuss the following:

- What are some ways you can bring Jesus into the conversation in your everyday lives? (*Talking about daily activities that revolve around Jesus, such as church, devotions, and so forth; talking about a recent story or talk you heard about Jesus; sharing a recent struggle and how you depended on Jesus; asking the other person about church, God or Jesus; talking about holidays—especially Christmas and Easter.*)

- What are some reactions you might receive? (*Interest, skepticism, disinterest, questions/debates, and sometimes straight-out rejection.*)

Close in prayer, giving students 30 seconds of silence (a rare event for the average junior-higher) to pray for someone who hasn't been healed by Jesus yet.

Option 2: Tag Teams. For this option, you need two volunteers (students or adults) who have helped each other learn to share about Jesus with others. Ahead of time, brainstorm with the volunteers and prepare a list of interview questions about how they work together to share about Jesus. Encourage the volunteers to be as specific as possible in their answers during the actual interview. Questions might include:

- How did you start working together to share about Jesus?
- What kinds of things do you do to help each of you know that you're working together?
- How have you learned together to share with others about your need for ongoing help from Jesus for your daily struggles and temptations?
- How has working together helped you in your efforts to share about Jesus?

Explain to the group that this is not the first time we've talked about sharing about Jesus with our friends, and although we've gotten better at it, we still need help. One of the reasons we don't share about Jesus with our friends is that we feel like we're alone when we do it and that today we're going to learn how we can make sharing about Jesus a team effort.

Introduce the volunteers and explain that they are going to discuss how they have worked together in sharing about Jesus. Conduct the interview, using the questions you prepared ahead of time; then discuss with the group: What are some ways that you could work with another person to share about Jesus with your friends? (*Praying for each other, praying together regularly, emailing each other encouraging reminders, starting a Christian club or Bible study on campus.*) Have students find partners and commit to doing one thing together to share their faith this week.

Point out to the group that it's not necessary for partners to attend the same school or live in the same area. There are many ways that students can partner together, including exchanging names of friends they're trying to share the gospel with and holding each other accountable through phone calls, texts or emails.

Ask partners to close in prayer, asking for boldness in their opportunities this week to share about Jesus.

REFLECT

The following short devotions are for the students to reflect on and answer during the week. You can make a copy of these pages and distribute to your class or download and print from **www.gospellight.com/uncommon/jh_ the_new_testament.zip.**

1—FOOT IN MOUTH DISEASE

If you've ever made a mistake or two of your own, run to John 21:15-17.

You couldn't believe the words were coming out of your mouth, but you couldn't stop yourself. Your best friend, Mel, had told you that she was tired of the way you gossiped about her. And yet there you were telling Gina that Mel liked Greg. You knew Mel was going to be mad at you, but you told Gina anyway. When Mel finds out, she might not even speak to you again.

The good news is that Jesus is not like Mel. Although He wants us to do the right thing, He forgives us when we blow it, even if we blow it over and over and over again. Look at how He forgave and reinstated Peter in John 21:15-17, even after Peter had denied knowing Him (see John 18:15-27).

Spend a few minutes confessing some of the things you've been doing that God doesn't want you to do, and thank Him for the way He forgives you, even when you keep making the same mistake. But don't stop there—ask Him to help you stop making that mistake!

2—WHAT I DON'T WANT TO DO, I DO

Race over to Romans 7:14-25.

"I just don't understand it," moans Davis. "I asked Jesus to be my Savior and take over my life, and I can tell that I'm a different person. But I still keep swearing, even though I try not to. Didn't Jesus take away all my sins?"

He's looking at you for an answer; what do you tell him?

If you're speechless, maybe you ask Davis to read Romans 7:14-25. Paul understood how tough it is to do the right thing, even though we've asked Jesus to be our Savior. But he gives us an answer in Romans 7:25. Reread it. Jesus will rescue us from our sins! It may take longer than we would expect or would like, but as we rely on Him, He will rescue us.

Is there a sin that you keep struggling with? If so, you need to keep asking Jesus to help you beat it. Spend a few minutes right now asking Him to help you do the right thing.

3—A LIFETIME OF GROWING

Hop and skip your way over to Philippians 1:3-6.

The weekend retreat had been great, and on Saturday night Diana stood up and said that she wanted to do a better job obeying and loving her parents. Unfortunately, by Tuesday, Diana was back to her old ways—at least some of them. Although she did a much better job cleaning her room when her parents asked her to do so, she still spent more time online talking with her friends than she spent talking to her parents. Even at dinner when her dad asked her how her day was, instead of telling him about the fight she saw at lunch or the cute guy who waved to her, she just said, "Fine," and kept on eating her meal.

Following Jesus often feels like we go three steps forward and two steps back. Diana had a powerful experience with God, and it made a difference in her life, but she still wasn't where she wanted to be.

The good news is that we have our whole lives to learn how to love and serve God and others. Today, thank God that He isn't impatient with you but is faithful to complete the good works that He began in you.

4—JUST LIKE GOD?

First Peter 1:13-16 is pretty cool. Go ahead—read it and see for yourself!

Charlie couldn't believe what he was reading in 1 Peter 1:13-16. Was God crazy or something? There's no way that he could be holy like God is holy. He was just a 13-year-old who struggled with cheating at school and looking at porn on the Internet. He wasn't holy. God must be out of His mind.

When Charlie met with his youth leader, Josh, to ask about these crazy verses, Josh told him that our holiness doesn't come from ourselves—it comes from Jesus and His forgiveness of our sins, which make us a new creation. But that doesn't mean we can coast through life. We need to cooperate with God as He transforms us more and more into His image, making us holy.

What is the sin that you are struggling with (see Day 2 devotion)? Ask God to help you be more holy in this one thing *today*. Since it takes a while to develop a habit, it will take a while to change a sinful habit or attitude; be prepared to ask Him for help again tomorrow and the next day.

Read Philippians 1:6 and be encouraged. He has promised to complete His work in you.

GET TO KNOW
THE FOUR GOSPELS

Through these six sessions, you've gotten to know some people who had life-changing encounters with Jesus. Their stories are recorded in the part of the New Testament that we call the Four Gospels—the Gospels of Matthew, Mark, Luke and John. "Gospel" means "good news," and these books are all versions of the Good News of Jesus, written by four different believers.

Reading and studying the Gospels is the best way to find out about Jesus' life, ministry, death and resurrection. Each Gospel highlights different aspects of Jesus, and getting to know them will bring Jesus to life in your heart and mind. Here is a summary of what each Gospel writer was inspired to emphasize in his version of Jesus' life story.[1]

The Gospel According to Matthew
Matthew was one of Jesus' disciples. After Jesus' resurrection and ascension into heaven, Matthew ministered among Jewish Christians and his Gospel emphasizes the "Jewishness" of Jesus. Matthew wanted to assure his faith community that Jesus was Israel's promised Messiah, the Anointed One God had promised through the Old Testament prophets. To accomplish this goal, Matthew detailed Jesus' family history and quoted many of the Old Testament prophecies that predicted the coming Savior.

The Gospel According to Mark

Mark (or John Mark, as he is called in the book of Acts) was an early convert to Christianity who was close to Peter, one of Jesus' disciples. The version of Jesus' life in his Gospel is likely based on Peter's eye-witness accounts. Mark's goal was to emphasize Jesus as the Suffering Servant. His story jumps right into Jesus' ministry, and we see Him teaching and healing people, demonstrating God's desire to make people whole both spiritually and physically. His sacrifice on the cross, recounted in excruciating detail, shows the ultimate act of servanthood.

The Gospel According to Luke

Luke was a Greek physician who traveled with the apostle Paul on some of his missionary journeys. He also wrote the book of Acts. Luke wrote both books to another Greek, Theophilus, and emphasized the perfect humanity of Jesus, who is often called the "Son of Man" in Luke's Gospel. Jesus is shown to identify with our sorrows and trials in order to offer us the priceless gift of salvation. Luke highlighted Jesus' emotions and relationships to demonstrate that He was human, just like us.

The Gospel According to John

John was another of Jesus' disciples, and wrote his Gospel near the end of his life. While Luke emphasized Jesus' humanity in his Gospel, John sought to emphasize Jesus' divinity by showing that He was the Son of God. John structured his Gospel around seven "I am" statements made by Jesus, pointing his readers back to God's revelation of Himself to Moses: "I am who I am" (Exodus 3:14). John didn't want his readers to have any doubts about the Second Person of the Trinity: Jesus, God's Son.

Now that you've got a picture of each Gospel's portait of Jesus, plan to read them all during the next 40 days. Yes, really! Start with Matthew's Gospel and read three chapters per day through Mark, Luke and John. Get together with a friend to read during lunch at school, or meet with your small group during the week to encourage each other to keep up the good work. You can do it! Get to know Jesus like you never have before.

UNIT II

The Kingdom of God Is Growing

I remember one of the first times I felt like I was a part of a gathering that resembled the Early Church. There was a sense of expectancy—a commitment to authenticity. There was an awareness of supernatural help and comfort.

But it didn't happen at church. In fact, it wasn't even with a group of Christians. It was in an Alcoholics Anonymous meeting!

I had been invited to observe by a Christian friend of mine who had been attending AA for months. In this group, she had discovered comfort, understanding and a sense of divine empowerment that exceeded what she had experienced at her local church.

I walked away from that meeting excited about the hope and relationships that those people had, but saddened that the empowering community my friend had longed for was found *outside* her congregation.

When have you experienced gatherings that felt like the church described in the book of Acts? Hopefully, it's a regular experience for you and the others who worship with you in your church or ministry, but if we're honest, the church has lost much of its original passion and commitment. The sense of being over-our-heads-and-completely-lost-without-God has been replaced by self-reliance and self-sufficiency born of our own pride and sometimes fueled by the amazing training and equipping resources around us. Hours and hours of seeking God through prayer have been replaced by quick "Lord, please bless me, my family and my ministry" prayerettes we send up to God in the shower in the morning or on our drive to work or church. Honest, vulnerable and authentic relationships have been replaced by quick "Hello, how are you? . . . I'm fine, thank you," exchanges in church hallways and classrooms.

Not only have we lost out, but also so has the world around us. God's method of incarnational ministry—modeled in His Son, continued on in the book of Acts and reenacted in pockets of the Church today—is still impacting nonbelievers across all continents. But does anyone really believe that we are reaching our full potential? No. We have substituted neatly packaged religion for radical, costly Christianity—and the non-believing world around us sees only glimpses of God's original plan for discipleship and evangelism.

We've geared this unit toward one simple goal: to help students realize that the same power unleashed in the Early Church is available to them today. Here are two fundamental ways you can reinforce what we've tried to communicate in these six lessons:

1. **Have a new biblical norm.** Please don't let your students grow up thinking that the way they experience church in this century is the way God intended it (unless, of course, you're in one of those unique churches that really is moving in the power of the Spirit and seeing God-sized results). Reinforce that God's plan, as outlined in the New Testament, is far superior to all other preconceptions we have about the nature and function of the Church. (*One note:* It's not just your students, but in all likelihood also you—and most definitely me—who need to recalibrate our understanding based on God's model of Church rather than on our own experiences.)

2. **Allow the Holy Spirit to control the meeting.** As much time as we, and now you, will spend preparing for these lessons, you can't know for sure what God is going to do. He's God, after all. If we could understand Him and anticipate His every move, He'd be more like a cool guy than the holy God. What that means is that you have the chance to remain sensitive to every prodding, leading and nudging of the Holy Spirit as He works in your students' lives in ways that you can't quite expect. The question from that rowdy seventh-grade boy who seems like a tangent may be just the door the Holy Spirit wants your students to walk through.

Now, enjoy the adventure, and may the qualities of the leaders and the power of the Holy Spirit found in the Early Church infect your life and be contagious to your students.

Kara Powell
Executive Director of the Fuller Youth Institute
Assistant Professor of Youth, Family and Culture
Fuller Theological Seminary

EMPOWERED BY THE HOLY SPIRIT

THE BIG IDEA

The Holy Spirit gives us power to be effective witnesses for Jesus to the world.

SESSION AIMS

In this session you will guide students to (1) see that the Church began through the power of the Holy Spirit; (2) feel confident that His power is still at work in the Church today; and (3) accept the help of the Holy Spirit to make them God's witnesses this week.

THE BIGGEST VERSE

"God has raised this Jesus to life, and we are all witnesses of the fact. Exalted to the right hand of God, he has received from the Father the promised Holy Spirit and has poured out what you now see and hear" (Acts 2:32-33).

OTHER IMPORTANT VERSES

Exodus 3:2; 1 Kings 18:38; Isaiah 6:6-7; Luke 24:48-51; John 16:7; Acts 1:4-9; 2; Romans 1:16

Note: Additional options and worksheets in $8^1/_2$" x 11" format for this session are available for download at **www.gospellight.com/uncommon/jh_the_new_testament.zip**.

STARTER

Option 1: Fire Starter. For this option, you need your Bible, a bag of charcoal briquettes (not self-igniting, but the kind that need lighter fluid to ignite), a barbecue (or large metal container that will safely confine a fire), three large paper bags, lighter fluid and matches. Place an equal number of briquettes into each bag. (*Note:* You'll really be lighting a fire in the barbecue, so it's best to do this option outside! Also, you might want to save the hot briquettes after the activity to use them for making S'mores at the end of this session.)

Greet students and divide them into three equal teams. Instruct each team to line up single file facing the barbecue and sit down. Give a bag of briquettes to the last person on each team (the one farthest away from the barbecue) and explain the object of the game: to be the first team to get all of its briquettes into the barbecue. Too simple? You're right. Here's the catch: Teammates can use only their feet to pass the briquettes forward! Only the very last person in each team can use his or her hands to put the briquettes into the barbecue. (You may or may not want the students to take off their shoes to do this activity—it's up to you. If you go for it, have some wet wipes on hand to clean up!)

Stop the game when the first team gets all of its briquettes into the barbecue. Call students' attention to the barbecue as you take out a match and attempt to light a fire. Without putting any lighter fluid on the briquettes, take out a match and try to light them. You should have some difficulty getting a fire started—and that's good! Continue the attempt to light the fire without lighter fluid until someone points out that you need something besides matches to get the coals lit. (It shouldn't take too long for someone to point out your obvious lack of know-how!)

Pour the lighter fluid on the briquettes. While it's soaking in, explain that just as each team passed its briquettes forward, Christians have been given the job of passing on the message of Jesus to the people around us. But we still need something else to get the fire of faith going—power to light the fire! Carefully light the briquettes (hopefully you'll get a nice big flame!).

Continue by stating that the Bible calls that power the Holy Spirit—the third Person of the Trinity. His coming ignited a flame of faith in the hearts of the first Christians and continues to do the same for believers today. Ask a volunteer to read Acts 1:8, and then explain that during the next six weeks, we're going to take a look at that first Church and see how the power of the Holy Spirit made ordinary people powerful witnesses for Jesus Christ. The history of the Early Church is recorded in the New Testament book of Acts, while the Epistles of the New Testament, such as the letters to the Romans, Galatians and Ephesians, were written to help those early believers live out their faith together. As we study Acts and the New Testament letters, we not only learn about the history of the Church, but we also learn how we can live out our faith today.

Transition by stating that Jesus' death and resurrection were not the end of the story of Christianity but the beginning. Christians are called to carry on what Jesus began, bringing His message of forgiveness and reconciliation to the world. And with the power of the Holy Spirit, we can do it!

Option 2: Sequels. For this option, you need self-adhesive nametags, a felt-tip pen and candy or other goodies for prizes.

Before the meeting, think of as many teen-friendly movie series as you can. Write one movie title on each nametag, making sure you have one for each title in the series. For example, one set of nametags might be *Spider-Man, Spider-Man 2, Spider-Man 3*. Another could include *Raiders of the Lost Ark, Indiana Jones and the Temple of Doom; Indiana Jones and the Last Crusade* and *Indiana Jones and the Kingdom of the Crystal Skull*. Another might be *Star Wars, The Empire Strikes Back* and *Return of the Jedi*. (Other series, if appropriate for your group, could also include *X-Men, The Chronicles of Narnia* or *The Lord of the Rings*.) Make enough tags for each member of your group, plus a few extra for visitors. (It's okay to make duplicates if your group is larger than the number of movies you can think of.)

Greet students as they arrive and place a nametag on each person's back *without letting anyone see his or her own tag*. (Make sure no one tells anyone else what his or her tag says!) Begin the session by discussing the following:

- Who loves movies? (*Check the temperature of anyone who doesn't respond!*)
- What are some of your all-time favorite movies?
- Who thinks they know a lot about movie sequels?

Explain that on each nametag is the title of a movie or a movie sequel. At your signal, they are to read each others' nametags aloud and get into groups *in order*, according to the original movie and all its sequels. For example, if their nametag says *Star Wars*, they should look for the rest of the movies in that series and then get into order from the original movie to its latest sequel. (If there are duplicate series, have the students form separate groups.)

Signal for students to begin. After the confusion dies down and everyone has found a place in line, call the groups forward, one by one, and read all of the nametags in order. With the help of your junior high movie buffs, correct any mistakes and award prizes to everyone. Now discuss the following:

- A lot of people say that the sequel to a movie is never as good as the original. Do you agree? (*Sometimes; it depends upon the movie.*)
- What makes a good movie? (*Good plot, strong characters, creative endings, and so forth.*)
- What makes a good movie sequel? (*It has all the appeal of the original movie, but takes the plot and characters even further.*)
- If Jesus' life was the original movie, what would the sequel be? (*His Church—not the building, but the people who have come to God through faith in Him. This might be hard for the students to think of at first, but lead them along until they hit upon this idea.*)
- What do you think of when you hear the word "Christianity"? (*Jesus, religion, the Bible, church, and so forth.*)
- What do you think of when you hear the word "church"? (*This building, youth group, and so forth.*)

Explain that many times when we think of Christianity or the Church, we think only of Jesus and that He died on the cross for our sins—and that is the ground level of it all. But Jesus' death and resurrection were not the *end* of the story of Christianity; it was the *beginning*. In a sense, the Church is the sequel to the story of Jesus. The history of the Early Church is recorded in the New Testament book of Acts, while the Epistles of the New Testament, such as the letters to the Romans, Galatians and Ephesians, were written to help those early believers live out their faith together. As we study Acts and the New Testament letters, we not only learn about the history of the Church, but we also learn how we can live out our faith today.

We aren't adding to His message, but we are spreading His message to the people around us—ultimately passing it on to the next generation. Christians are called to carry on what Jesus began and bring His message of forgiveness and reconciliation to the world. And with the power of the Holy Spirit, we can do it!

Transition by stating that during the next six weeks, we're going to take a look at the first Church and see how the power of the Holy Spirit made ordinary people powerful witnesses for Jesus Christ.

MESSAGE

Option 1: Worth Waiting For. For this option, you need several Bibles, several washable felt-tip pens in various colors and several light-colored T-shirts, copies of "The Three *P*s of Pentecost" (found on the next page) and pens or pencils.

The Three Ps of Pentecost

The Promise

(Luke 24:48-49; Acts 1:4-9)

Ⓟ What did Jesus tell the disciples to do?

Ⓟ What would they receive?

Ⓟ What would this give them the ability to be?

The Power

(Acts 2:1-13)

Ⓟ What feast was being celebrated that day?

Ⓟ What three miraculous signs occurred when the Holy Spirit came?

Ⓟ What were the believers declaring?

The Proclamation

(Acts 2:14-18,32-41)

Ⓟ What did God promise to "pour out in the last days"?

Ⓟ What did Peter say the believers were (v. 32)?

Ⓟ How many people were added to the Church that day?

(*Optional:* You can use butcher paper or poster board taped to the wall instead of a T-shirt.)

Divide students into teams of four or five. (*Note:* Keep girls with girls and boys with boys for this one!) Give each team felt-tip pens and a T-shirt. On your signal, one team member must don the shirt, then the rest of the team must write a list of things that they wait for on the back of the T-shirt—pizza delivery, computer to boot up, cookies to come out of the oven, lines at amusement parks, and so on. After 60 seconds, signal the teams to stop. Read their lists and award the team with the most answers with a round of applause.

Explain that while sometimes we hate waiting for things, some things are really worth waiting for because of the benefit we receive when they finally arrive. One of the best examples of this is found in the book of Acts. Jesus had just spent 40 days talking with His disciples about God's kingdom, and right before He ascended into heaven, He told them to *wait* until they received something that would give them the power to be His witnesses: the Holy Spirit.[1]

Distribute Bibles, "The Three *P*s of Pentecost" and pens or pencils, and instruct students to work together to look up the Bible references and answer the questions. When all the groups have finished, come back together and discuss the students' answers. Ask a volunteer to read Luke 24:48-49 and Acts 1:4-9. Explain that Jesus' instructions were clear: The disciples were to wait until they received power. He knew that they would need the power of God to effectively take His message to the world. The power He was talking about was the Holy Spirit, the third member of the Trinity. Before they could be His witnesses, they needed to wait for the Holy Spirit to come.

Next, ask a volunteer to read Acts 2:1-13. Explain to the group that Pentecost was (and is) a Jewish holiday that celebrates God giving the Law, the Torah, to Moses on Mount Sinai. Many Jews from all over the Roman Empire were gathered in Jerusalem to celebrate Pentecost. It was during that time, 50 days after Jesus' resurrection, that the Holy Spirit came and filled the waiting disciples with the power to be Jesus' witnesses.

Three miraculous signs occurred when the Holy Spirit came: (1) A rushing wind filled the house; (2) flames of fire rested on each believer; and (3) they declared the wonders of God in languages they had never learned. These miracles were so amazing that people from all over the city came to see what had happened. This was the disciples' first opportunity to be witnesses for Jesus. And now the Holy Spirit had given the power to do it effectively.

Finally, ask a volunteer to read Acts 2:14-18,32-41. Conclude by stating that this event, which we even today celebrate as Pentecost, was the beginning of the Christian Church, and resulted in thousands being saved that very day. Peter and the other believers were effective witnesses because the power of the Holy Spirit was in them. Jesus had walked with them, but now the Holy Spirit was living in them—and all Jerusalem noticed!

Option 2: Famous Last Words. For this option, you just need this book.

Explain that after Jesus' resurrection, He appeared to His disciples and spent 40 days talking with them about the kingdom of God. Then, right before He went to be with the heavenly Father, He used His last words to make a promise to them. Ask volunteers to read Luke 24:48-51 and Acts 1:4-9, and ask the group: (1) What Jesus wanted His disciples to do (*stay in the city of Jerusalem until they received power*); and (2) Why they needed power from God (*to be witnesses of the things that they had seen.*)

Continue by stating that the disciples were going to continue Jesus' kingdom work, sharing with others God's plan of peace and forgiveness. But they couldn't do it on their own. To share God's message, they needed God's power. Have students briefly share what they think Jesus meant by "power," and then invite them to listen carefully as a volunteer reads Acts 2:1-4. Continue by discussing the following:

- The Holy Spirit came, just as Jesus promised. What three signs occurred when the Holy Spirit came? (*The disciples heard wind, saw fire and spoke in languages they had not learned.*)

- What did each of these signs mean? (*In general, the wind is felt to represent the presence of the Holy Spirit Himself; the tongues of fire show the cleansing and empowering work of the Spirit in the disciples; the languages were a supernatural gift of the Holy Spirit to enable the disciples to proclaim the gospel message to the whole world.*)

- How would these signs give the believers power to be witnesses? (*They were supernatural abilities that helped the believers tell others about Jesus.*)

Explain that Pentecost was and is a Jewish holiday that celebrates God giving the Law, the Torah, to Moses on Mount Sinai. Many Jews from all over the Roman Empire were gathered in Jerusalem to celebrate Pentecost, and these visiting Jews spoke many different languages. It was during that time, 50 days after Jesus' resurrection, that the Holy Spirit came and filled the waiting disciples with the power to be Jesus' witnesses.

State that the Church was born on that day. Now the disciples were able to bring Christ's message to the world—through the power of the Holy Spirit.

DIG

Option 1: Good Witness. For this option, you need a wild costume (a gorilla mask, clown shoes, a polka-dot necktie, flaming-red boxer shorts and a baseball bat—whatever you can find hanging around the church closets). Arrange for an adult volunteer to be dressed in the costume and ready to burst in on your group at the appropriate time.

Explain to the group that before Jesus ascended into heaven, He promised His disciples the gift of the Holy Spirit to give them power to be His witnesses. The Holy Spirit did come—the Day of Pentecost exploded with the power of His awesome presence. But is that same power still around today? Can we expect God to give us the power to be a witness, just like Peter and those first believers? Well, it all depends on what a person's idea of a witness is.

Discuss the following questions:

- What is a witness? (*Someone who tells others what they saw and heard.*)
- Have you ever been an official witness to something, such as an accident? What did you do? (*If none of the students have been official witnesses, tell them about a time when you were a witness, such as at a court case, traffic accident, school incident, wedding, and so forth.*)
- Can a witness choose what they want to say happened? (*No, their job is simply to tell what they experienced to the best of their ability.*)
- What gives someone the ability to be a witness? (*The fact that they have experienced something firsthand.*)

Have a volunteer read 2 Peter 1:16 and 1 John 1:1, and then discuss why the disciples were able to be witnesses for Jesus. (*They had personally experienced the love and power for Jesus. They told what they had seen and heard.*) Continue to lead students in a discussion about what a witness is until the volunteer bursts into the room. The volunteer should run through the meeting area for about 10 seconds, making a lot of noise and commotion, and then exit.

After students have calmed down, say, "Wow! What was that? I've never seen that happen before!" Begin to *incorrectly* describe what you saw, giving the students a chance to show they were paying attention by correcting your mistakes. When a true description has been reached, ask the group the following:

- Who were the most effective witnesses? (*Those who were in the room and paying attention.*)

- Could someone in the next room be as effective a witness as you have been? Why? (*No, because they weren't here to experience it themselves. They could only give a secondhand account.*)

- How does this idea relate to being witnesses for Jesus? (*If we have a personal relationship with Jesus and are focused on Him by reading the Bible and spending daily time in prayer, then we will know the truth more clearly and tell it to others more effectively.*)

- But why do we need the power of the Holy Spirit to be witnesses? Can't we just say what we know? (*That's just it: without the Holy Spirit we would never know! The Bible says that spiritual things can only be understood as the Spirit reveals them to us. Without the Holy Spirit, our eyes would forever be closed to the truth of who Jesus is and what He has done for us—see 1 Corinthians 2:9-14; Ephesians 1:17.*)

Conclude by stating that when we are tuned in to the Lord, relying on the power of the Holy Spirit to help us know Jesus better, we are able to be witnesses of Jesus Christ to others. A witness does what we just did—tell the truth about what he or she has seen and heard. When a person comes to know Jesus Christ—when he or she really encounters His presence and the power of His Holy Spirit—then that person is able to effectively share Christ with those around him or her. Just like the believers on the Day of Pentecost, the Holy Spirit wants to fill us with His power.

Option 2: Firsthand Knowledge. For this option, you need this case study.

There once was a Shakespearean actor who was known far and wide for his one-man show of readings and recitations from the classics. He would always end his performances with a dramatic reading of the Twenty-third Psalm. Each night, without exception, as the actor began his recitation: "The Lord is my shepherd, I shall not want" the crowd would listen attentively. And then, at the conclusion of the psalm, they would rise in thunderous applause in appreciation of the actor's incredible ability to bring the verse to life.

But one night, just before the actor was to offer his customary recital of the Twenty-third Psalm, a young man from the audience spoke up. "Sir, do you mind if tonight I recite the Twenty-third Psalm?"

The actor was quite taken aback by this unusual request, but he allowed the young man to come forward and stand front and center on the stage to recite the psalm, knowing that the ability of this unskilled youth would be of no match for his own talent.

With a soft voice, the young man began to recite the words of the psalm. When he finished there was no applause. There was no standing ovation as on other nights. All that could be heard was the sound of weeping. The audience was so moved by the young man's recitation, that every eye was full of tears.

Amazed by what he heard, the actor said to the youth, "I don't understand. I have been performing the Twenty-third Psalm for years. I have a lifetime of experience and training—but I have never been able to move an audience as you have tonight. Tell me, what is your secret?"

The young man humbly replied, "Well, sir, you know the psalm, but I know the Shepherd."[2]

Next, discuss the following:

- Have you ever tried to explain something that you didn't understand from firsthand experience? Were you able to share with confidence? (*If students can't think of anything, remind them about when they have given oral reports on topics they knew well, as opposed to topics teachers randomly assigned.*)

- How can this idea relate to our experience with Jesus? (*Knowing Him firsthand through the power of the Holy Spirit gives us the ability to share effectively with others about what He has done. We aren't just telling what we've read, but also what we've experienced.*)

- Why do we need the power of the Holy Spirit to be witnesses for Jesus? Can't we just say what we know? (*That's just it—without the Holy Spirit we would* never *know! The Bible says that spiritual things can only be understood as the Spirit reveals them to us. Without the Holy Spirit, our eyes would forever be closed to the truth of who Jesus is and what He has done for us—see 1 Corinthians 2:9-14; Ephesians 1:17.*)

Conclude by stating that just like the believers on the Day of Pentecost, the Holy Spirit wants to fill us with His power. He wants to give us a firsthand experience that will change us forever and make us effective witnesses for Jesus Christ.

APPLY

Option 1: What's the Difference? For this option, you need your Bible, copies of "What's the Difference?" (found on the next page), pens or pencils and worship music (live or recorded).

Distribute Bibles, "What's the Difference?" and pens or pencils. Explain that when we talk about witnessing, we are tempted to turn it into an activity instead of what it really is—an outgrowth of our relationship with Jesus. Divide students into groups of four or five and instruct them to complete their handouts. Allow a few minutes, and then have students share within their groups which of the verses seem the most significant to them at this moment in their lives.

Continue by stating that when the Holy Spirit comes to live in us, we become a different person—we become someone who exemplifies the Lord. Does this mean we become perfect? No, but it does mean an obvious change of heart that happens through the power of the Holy Spirit.

Have students remain in their small groups and pray for each other that they would have power through the Holy Spirit to be bold witnesses in word *and* deed, becoming more like Jesus daily. Read Acts 1:8 and close with a time of worship, exalting God and praising His goodness and grace.

Option 2: Prayerwalk. For this option, you need the power of the Holy Spirit and some adult volunteers.

As an immediate extension of this session, prepare for a short prayerwalk around the church facility or meeting place. Explain to the group that sometimes our witness for Jesus isn't a speech to others. We can bring the influence of the kingdom of God simply by being somewhere and praying, by the power of the Holy Spirit, for God's will to be done in that place. Today we are going to be witnesses by praying for God's power to come to our church so that, as we read in Acts 2, many people will be drawn to a relationship with God through Jesus Christ.

Divide students into groups of three or four and assign each group an adult volunteer and a particular area of the church grounds to prayerwalk. Have students pray for an outpouring of God's power among the people of your congregation. Return and have a time of worship—and, if you used option 1 in the Starter section, those delicious, long awaited S'mores!

What's the Difference?

2 Corinthians 5:17
When I give my life to Christ, I become a

_____ _____.

Ephesians 4:24
As a Christian, my new self is created to be like God
in _____ and true _____.

1 Corinthians 6:19
I am a temple of the _____ _____.

1 Peter 3:15
As a witness I should be prepared to give an answer for
the _____ that is in me.

REFLECT

The following short devotions are for the students to reflect on and answer during the week. You can make a copy of these pages and distribute to your class or download and print from **www.gospellight.com/uncommon/jh_the_new_testament.zip.**

1—GIVE AN ANSWER

Visit John 14:26.

Greg was sipping on a soda in the mall when Fred—the most popular guy in school—walked up and said hi. Greg was shocked, since he and Fred hadn't talked since third grade. Fred asked Greg if he had seen a certain movie on TV last Wednesday night. Greg answered that he hadn't seen it and then explained that Wednesday is the night he goes to church for youth group. Fred was curious and started firing questions to Greg about God, and Greg was surprised that he was able to answer them. As they said goodbye, Greg asked Fred if he would like to come with him to church that Wednesday and Fred said yes.

God is *way* too big for us to remember everything about Him, but He has given us the Holy Spirit to help us learn and store away a bunch of what the Bible says. Right here, right now, thank God for sending the Holy Spirit and ask Him to make your mind like a sponge that absorbs as much as the Holy Spirit sends your way.

2—POSSIBLE OR IMPOSSIBLE?

Open up the Word and check out Mark 6:45-56.

Mark each statement with either *P* for "Possible" or *I* for "Impossible," depending on what you think you could do.

___ Bake 100 chocolate chip cookies.
___ Win the gold medal on the vert ramp in the X Games.
___ Get straight *A*s for an entire year.
___ Bench-press 300 pounds.
___ Invite the most popular kid at school to church.

Guess what? Even the things that we think are impossible for us to do are possible for God to do! And that includes seeing anyone and everyone on your campus come to know Him as Savior. And get this: He might even work through you to reach them.

Who are the impossible people in your life? Ask God to help you make it possible for them to know and love Him.

3—POWER TO MAKE A DIFFERENCE

Use only your pinkie fingers and turn to Ephesians 3:20-21.

Cindy was the captain of the volleyball team. During her eighth-grade season, Cindy set all of the school records. Volleyball took a lot of time, but she was able to remain active in church as well as earn great grades.

Cindy made a commitment at camp last summer to share Christ with her volleyball teammates. Although none of them have become Christians yet, three of them attend church with her regularly.

Do you know anyone like Cindy? Someone who seems able to do everything right? Well, guess what? When we have God in our lives, we are able to do more things for Him than we could ever think possible. God wants to use you to do things that have never been done before. When God uses you for His glory, it's impossible to measure what will happen.

Tell God right now that you want to be used for Him. Ask God to dump His power on you so that you can make a difference.

4—CHANGE AWAITS!

On your marks . . . get set . . . go to 1 Samuel 10:6.

If you could change one thing about the following people, what would it be?

Your math teacher: _____

Your best friend: _____

Your pet (or your brother or sister!): _____

When God gets hold of people, they change. God has the ability to change people who might have done some rotten things and make them new creations. That means we are all new creations made to do great things for God.

But have you ever known someone who calls himself or herself a Christian but has not really been changed? Or maybe that's you. Ask God today to change you into a new creation made for Him. As you go through your day, remember that you are that new creation who is able to do all things for God!

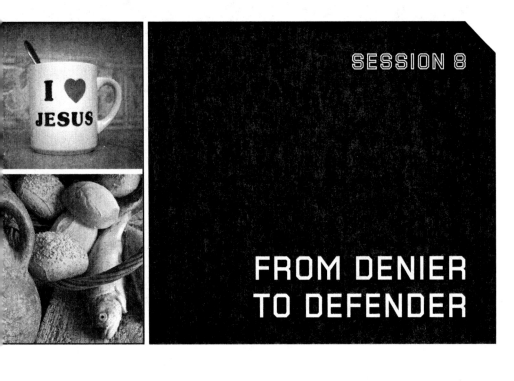

FROM DENIER
TO DEFENDER

THE BIG IDEA

Through the power of the Holy Spirit, even flawed people can be bold witnesses for Jesus.

SESSION AIMS

In this session you will guide students to (1) see that weakness does not mean failure; (2) realize that the power of the gospel is in the message, not the messenger; and (3) feel the encouragement of the Holy Spirit to speak boldly as witnesses for Jesus.

THE BIGGEST VERSE

"I am not ashamed of the gospel, because it is the power of God for the salvation of everyone who believes" (Romans 1:16).

OTHER IMPORTANT VERSES

Matthew 26:69-75; John 2:11; Acts 1:8; 1 Corinthians 2:3-4; 2 Corinthians 3:4-6; 1 Thessalonians 1:5; 1 John 1:7-9

Note: Additional options and worksheets in 8^1/$_2$" x 11" format for this session are available for download at **www.gospellight.com/uncommon/jh_the_new_testament.zip**.

STARTER

Option 1: Verse Scramble Relay. For this option, you need several Bibles, paper, a felt-tip pen, three rolls of transparent tape, and candy or other goodies for prizes. Ahead of time, create three sets of the entire Romans 1:16 verse, one word per slip of paper; then scramble the word order and spread each set face down on the floor near a wall. (*Note:* Be sure to keep each set together, even while scrambled!)

Greet students and review the main ideas from the previous session:

- How many of you were able to be a witness for Jesus during this past week? (*Encourage students to share ways in which they not only spoke the gospel but also lived it in their actions and attitudes.*)

- Why do we need the Holy Spirit's help to be witnesses? (*Through the power of the Holy Spirit, we experience a relationship with God—just like the believers experienced on the Day of Pentecost—and then can tell others what we know with firsthand testimony.*)

Transition to this session by asking what happens when we are lousy witnesses and make a mess of sharing the gospel. (*We feel guilty; we feel that God is disappointed in us; we quit trying to be witnesses.*) Explain that there are many examples of God turning people's total failures into awesome miracles in His name. If we don't give up, God can turn everything around for good. It is not our ability that matters, but His message!

Ask a volunteer to read Romans 1:16. Have students repeat the verse three or four times so they get a feel for the word order. Make sure the students catch the middle part of this verse by stating the following: "What is the power of God for salvation? The gospel. Not a church, not a preacher, not good works—the gospel is the power of God for the salvation of everyone who believes!"

Divide students into three teams and assign each team a "verse wall." Explain that on the floor are the words to Romans 1:16. One at a time, team members will run to their team's wall, pick up a piece of paper, read it and tape it to the wall—then run back and sit down so the next person in line can go. The first team to get the verse taped to the wall in the correct order wins.

Two rules: Students must use the first paper they pick up and they can only rearrange the words after all of them have been taped up. Depending on the number of students on each team, each student might need to go up two or three times.

Award prizes to the winning team. Conclude by stating that our goal as believers in Jesus is to pass on His message to those around us. We can only do this through the power of the Holy Spirit. Today we're going to read about a man who went from denying Jesus to defending Him. God used this man to do miraculous things that brought thousands of Jews to Christ because the power of the gospel is in the message, not the messenger!

Option 2: Beggars. For this option, you need a really appealing junior-high food item (such as fast-food burger, an ice-blended mocha or a smoothie) and a paper bag. Hide the food item in the bag.
Greet students and review last week's session:

- How many of you had the opportunity to be a witness for Jesus this past week? (*Choose a few students to share.*)
- Who gives us the power to be witnesses? (*The Holy Spirit.*)

Let students know that you're going to play a game and select three volunteers who claim to be *really* good at begging—the kind of begging that can get cows to fly, even if they don't want to! Have a 15-second warm-up for contestants to prime their begging pumps (shaking out their arms and legs, jumping jacks, cracking knuckles, and so on), and then remove the food item from the bag. Allow each contestant to beg for the food (you can wave it in front of their noses for added effect) and have the audience gauge his or her effectiveness by applause. Declare a winner by the contestant who gets the most applause, and award him or her the food.
Conclude by explaining that you're going to learn about three miracles—including one that happened to a beggar—that God performed through someone who totally failed and messed up as a witness for Jesus. This person should have given up Christianity and become a hermit; instead, God used him to do amazing things.

MESSAGE

Option 1: Eyewitness Report. For this option, you need several Bibles, three copies of "Eyewitness Report" (found on the next page), and pens or pencils.
Read Acts 4:33. Explain that after the believers had received the power of the Holy Spirit to witness for Jesus, many wonderful miracles occurred through them. Miracles are one way that the Holy Spirit uses us to be witnesses, because

Eyewitness Report

Circle your group's assigned miracle passage and read the verses in your Bible. Write down the key information from the passage, including as many specific details as you can.

	Acts 3:1-10	Acts 5:1-11	Acts 5:12-32
Who:			
What:			
When:			
Where:			
Why:			
Result:			

miracles reveal God's glory so that people can put their faith in Him (see John 2:11). Today, we are going to read about three specific miracles done through Peter—one of Jesus' disciples who had only a few months earlier denied Jesus in front of everyone (see Matthew 26:69-75). This denier became an incredible witness of Jesus in the Early Church because the Holy Spirit had changed his heart and filled him with boldness and power.[1]

Divide students into three groups and distribute Bibles, one copy of "Eyewitness Report," and a pen or pencil to each group. Assign each group one of the Scripture passages (Acts 3:1-10; Acts 5:1-11; Acts 5:12-32) from the handout and instruct groups to read their assigned passage and complete the handout, then come up with a way to communicate what they read. (This could take the form of an on-the-spot interview with a main character, talk show, news broadcast, a reenactment, and so forth.) Everyone in each group should have a part in the presentation.

After the groups have presented their passages, continue by stating that these awesome miracles did not happen through Peter because he was perfect or smart or educated—in fact, from Acts 4:13 we know that he wasn't any of those things. God used Peter because he was open to being used. It wasn't Peter; it was Jesus! Even deniers can become defenders. It is the power of the gospel message that changes lives, not the power of the messenger.

Option 2: The Power Behind the Miracles. For this option, you need two adult volunteers, copies of "The Power Behind the Miracles" (found on the next page), a desk (or small table), four chairs and some upbeat music such as used on *The Tonight Show*. (*Note:* This option will take some advanced preparation, but if done well, it is something the students will remember for a long time!)

Set up the front of the room to look like the set of a late-night talk show (a desk off to the side, four chairs lined up in a row, and so forth). Give the volunteers copies of the skit and have at least one rehearsal prior to the session.

Introduce the skit by explaining that you've arranged for the group members to attend the taping of a late-night talk show. After the performance, explain that they read the whole story (plus a little more) in Acts 3–6. These awesome miracles did not happen through Peter, one of Jesus' disciples, because he was perfect or smart or educated—in fact, we know that he wasn't any of those things. He had once openly denied Jesus! God used Peter as an incredible witness to the good news because he was open to being used. It wasn't Peter; it was Jesus! It is the power of the gospel message that changes lives, not the power of the messenger.

The *POWER* Behind the Miracles

The Cast: Host, Peter
The Props: A desk, four chairs, upbeat instrumental music (and a way to play it)

Host: (*Play music as the host is coming out and greeting the audience—an ad-lib joke or two would be appropriate.*) Welcome! We have a fantastic lineup of guests tonight, so let's get started! (*Take a seat at the desk.*) My first guest was one of the original 12 disciples of Jesus. A former fisherman, he left it all to follow Jesus. My guest suffered a chronic case of foot-in-mouth disease for a while, but lately he's been doing incredible—and I mean incredible—miracles. Put your hands together and give it up for the apostle to the Jews, the defender of the faith, the miracle-man himself—

Peter: (*Running out and interrupting the introduction.*) Stop! Stop! You've got it all wrong! I am nothing but an ordinary man—

Host: Ordinary? (*Looks amused.*) How can you say that? You're Peter! You've healed the lame, cast out demons—

Peter: No! It wasn't me . . . I didn't do any of that!

Host: What? (*Looking perplexed.*) Aren't you the apostle Peter?

Peter: Yes, but—

Host: Haven't you seen hundreds of awesome miracles?

Peter: Yes, but—

Host: Didn't you heal a lame beggar while you were on your way to the Temple?

Peter: Well, I was there, but—

Host: (*Interrupting.*) Imposter! (*Looking around, shouting to stage hands.*) Get this guy outta here! (*To the audience, attempting to look composed.*) I'm sorry about this, we'll get everything settled and—

Peter: (*Interrupting.*) Wait! Please! Let me explain!

Host: Okay, you have 20 seconds.

Peter: I was on my way to the Temple for prayer with my friend John. As we entered the gate called Beautiful, I saw a lame beggar asking for money. I know he'd probably been there before, but this day I really saw him.

Host: Uh-huh, I see. So that's when you healed him, right?

Peter: Not exactly. When I saw him sitting there, the power of the Holy Spirit rose up inside me and I felt the boldness of the Lord. I told the beggar, "I don't have any money, but I'll give you what I do have—the name of Jesus. Get up and walk!"

Host: What happened?

Peter: I reached down to that lame beggar and grabbed his hand, and immediately his legs and ankles were strong again. He jumped up and began dancing all around. It was amazing! People who saw it were astounded, because this man hadn't walked for more than 40 years!

Host: Then you did heal him! (*Going back to his original enthusiasm.*) You are the miracle man, apostle to the Jews, defender of—

Peter: No! No! It wasn't me at all. I don't have any special power. I'm just an ordinary man; it was faith in the name of Jesus that brought the miracle. It's God's message about Jesus that has the power to change people's lives, not the messenger. I am only a witness of what Jesus said and did.

Host: Oh, I get it! (*Chuckles and winks at audience.*) You're being humble.

Peter: No, no, that's not it at all. I am not being humble—just honest. Let me tell you something about my past. When I was one of Jesus' 12 disciples, I swore to His face that I would never leave Him. That no matter what, I would stick with Him.

Host: How bold! How holy! How—

Peter: (*Interrupting and completing the host's sentence.*) How untrue!

Host: What? How can you say that?

Peter: Because not too long after that promise, Jesus was arrested and I denied three times that I even knew Him.

Host: (*Stunned for a minute.*) You . . . you denied Jesus?

Peter: I did. I was afraid of what would happen to me and I denied Him.

Host: Well, then shouldn't you be on the doesn't-deserve-to-be-used-by-God list, or something, instead of being able to perform miracles?

Peter: Yes, I should be. But that's not how it works. God completely changed me through the power of His Holy Spirit. He cleansed me of my sins and gave me true boldness to be a witness for Jesus. Now when I tell others about Him, I speak from firsthand experience. I know the gospel message has changed me—and that it can change absolutely anyone!

Host: So the miracles are not because of your power, but because of the power of God working through you? You're just giving to others what you have received?

Peter: Exactly!

Host: Well, it looks like we're coming to a station break, so we'll have to stop for now. Let's give a hand for my guest. Coming up next, we'll talk to Bob the camel seller—stay tuned!

DIG

Option 1: I Bow Down. For this option, you need several Bibles, a clear pitcher filled with water, at least two clear glasses, the song "I Bow Down" off the Audio Adrenaline CD titled *Underdog* (download it off iTunes or some other online music store or pick up the CD), and a way to play the track.

Begin by explaining that when the apostle Paul wrote his letters to the Corinthian church, who lived in the ancient city of Corinth, he was responding to major problems there. The Corinthians thought that in order to be a good leader—and a good person for that matter—you had to demonstrate superior wisdom and power. Paul's view of leadership flips that idea upside-down and paints a picture of leadership through weakness.

Distribute Bibles and ask volunteers to read the following verses: 1 Corinthians 2:3-4; 2 Corinthians 3:4-6; 4:7; 12:9-10; 1 Thessalonians 1:5. After the students have read these verses, discuss the following:

- What do all these verses have in common? (*They all talk about where our strength to witness and be a follower of Jesus comes from—God.*)
- When we consider our weaknesses, we often feel ashamed. Why? (*Because we are trained to think that we should be perfect, good and strong and never have any struggles. If we do struggle, we feel like we're weird or defective.*)
- Is weakness really bad? (*Not at all! It is just an area that needs to be touched by the power of God.*)
- What do these verses say about weaknesses? (*They are an opportunity for God's power to shine through.*)
- Why would God want to use weak, flawed people? (*To show that the power comes from Him.*)
- What does this say about God's ability to use us? (*Our weaknesses are the very places that God can reveal His glory and grace.*)

Demonstrate this with the water pitcher and glasses. As you pour water from the pitcher into the glass, explain that God is the pitcher and we are the glass. Next, as you pour water from one glass into the other (representing yet another person), state that this water that you are pouring ultimately came from God. God can work through us in a similar way. We open the door to God's power by surrendering our lives to Him and trusting in Him to strengthen and empower us. We boast in our weaknesses, realizing that those empty places can be filled with His power.

Ask the students to listen carefully to the lyrics as you play the song "I Bow Down." (*Note:* If the lyrics are difficult for the group to understand just by listening, read the lyrics aloud before the discussion.) At the conclusion of the song, discuss the following:

- What is this song saying? (*That when we bow down—lay our lives before God in complete surrender—God can lift us up.*)
- Have you ever seen God work through you when you were at a very low point? (*Encourage some personal stories, and be prepared with one of your own to share as well.*)
- What made the difference? (*Knowing that the power to witness and follow Jesus comes from the Holy Spirit, not us. We don't have to drum anything up. We simply rest in faith.*)

Transition by stating that the Holy Spirit came to give us the power we need to be witnesses. Just like we've seen in Peter, as well as in the water glass demonstration, when we rely on Him, He can work in us and through us to reveal God to others. God isn't looking for perfect people to be His witnesses. He wants people who have bowed down in surrender and experienced firsthand His power to save.

Option 2: Surprising Witness. For this option, you need just this book!
Share the following story:

Jessie closed her Bible, let out a sigh and argued with herself. *I know I'm supposed to tell others about Jesus, but I just can't. I'm too shy to stand up on a table in the middle of the quad and start preaching to the school. It's not that I don't love God; I just don't have the gift of evangelism.* She grabbed her books and headed out the door to catch the bus for school.

On the way to the bus stop, she found a beautiful silver bracelet. She picked it up and looked around to see if anyone was near. A woman was standing a few yards ahead of her. Jessie approached her and asked if she owned a silver bracelet. The woman looked at her wrist and realized that she was missing a bracelet. Jessie gave it to the woman and went on to the bus stop.

During school, one of her friends needed help with a math problem he just couldn't solve. Jessie spent her lunch break going over the problem with him and helping him get his homework done.

After school, her neighbor called and wanted Jessie to come and watch her two little girls so she could run to the store for milk. Jessie went and even did the dishes while she was there.

Before she went to sleep, Jessie thought again about being a witness. *I guess I just don't have what it takes to tell others about Jesus.*

Discuss the following:

- Why does Jessie feel discouraged about being a witness? (*Because to her, witnessing only means preaching to a group of people.*)
- Did Jessie share the gospel with others? (*Yes, through her kindness and helpfulness she showed her love for God.*)
- Was Jessie as weak a witness as she felt she was? (*No, she was actually giving a strong witness for the love of God.*)
- Saint Francis of Assisi once said, "Preach the gospel always; if necessary, use words." What did he mean? (*Our actions should be the greatest witness to our faith in Jesus.*)
- So wait a minute—are our words important at all? (*You bet they are, but our words and our actions should both point people to Jesus.*)
- If you think about witnessing in this way, how were you a witness for Jesus this past week? (*Allow for responses.*)

APPLY

Option 1: Flawed but Usable. For this option, you need swatches of flawed fabric and an elder or pastor from your church. Ask the leader to be ready to share a story of how he or she has seen God work in the midst of his or her flaws and weaknesses. (*Note:* This not only connects the students to the adult leadership of the church, but also gives the pastoral team a chance to stand with

Youth Leader Tip
Junior-highers tend to be self-conscious, so when choosing a volunteer, choose someone suited for the situation. Also try to provide a variety of opportunities so that those who are eager to be involved can participate in positive ways.

you in faith that God's plan is being done in and through the junior-highers of your church.)

Explain that being a Christian doesn't mean that you have to be perfect. What it does mean is that we have personally experienced the life-changing power of God and are in the process of learning how to love Him, follow Him and be His witnesses.

Invite your guest to come forward and share his or her story. Afterward, distribute a swatch of flawed fabric to each student. Explain that looking at this piece of fabric, we can see all the inconsistencies and flaws in its weave. But as we just heard, it can still be used for a good purpose.

Invite students to open the weakest areas of their lives to the power of the Holy Spirit. Wherever they struggle the most (lying, gossiping, fear, bad language, whatever), they should ask God to fill those weak areas with His power so that they can become areas that shine with the testimony of God's faithfulness and grace. Close in a time of individual or group prayer.

Option 2: Be Bold! You will need a whiteboard and a dry-erase marker.

Explain that Jesus said that the Holy Spirit has come to give us power to be His witnesses. As we will read today, the miracles that God did through Peter and the other believers resulted in many people coming to faith in Jesus. And that's what it is all about! There are many ways in which we can tell others what we know to be true about Jesus.

Have students call out practical ways they can be witnesses at school, at home and in their neighborhoods. Write down their suggestions on the whiteboard. Next, choose one or two of the ideas and challenge the students by stating something like the following: "Most of these ideas are things we can easily do. How can we stretch ourselves to think of something that we could only accomplish through the power of God?" Encourage the students to think beyond the norm. For example, if one idea was to help a friend with his or her schoolwork, you could take it a step further by suggesting a weekly homework club to help ESL (English as a Second Language) students from the neighborhood.

The idea is to stretch the group members—reasonably—and have them think of new ways to be an influence for the kingdom of God. Have students choose one idea to do within the next four weeks. Explain that during the last session of this unit, you'll give them a chance to share how God used them as they stepped out to be His witnesses.

Conclude by praying that God would give the students boldness and courage to be powerful (though never perfect) witnesses for Jesus Christ.

REFLECT

The following short devotions are for the students to reflect on and answer during the week. You can make a copy of these pages and distribute to your class or download and print from **www.gospellight.com/uncommon/jh_the_new_testament.zip.**

1—IN YOUR WEAKNESS, HE IS STRONG

Exodus 4:10-12 is sweet! So hurry up and check it out.

Moses was not a good public speaker. (I bet he used to break out in hives!) He knew that doing what God wanted him to do would be hard for him to pull off—and so he had to learn to trust God for everything.

The same thing happened to Heidi. Heidi was not a very good dancer, but when the church play needed dancers, Heidi was asked to dance. After thinking about it, she said yes, but she asked God to help her. She ended up being one of the best dancers in the whole play.

Many of us think that we are bad at telling people about Jesus. That is right where God wants us! He wants us to leave plenty of room for Him to work so that when we do tell people about Jesus, we know that He helped us. So let God know what is hard for you when it comes to telling people about Him, and then ask Him to give you a chance today to share anyway!

2—NO MORE HEART OF STONE

Have you ever read anything in Ezekiel? Go check out Ezekiel 36:25-28. It rips.

Check the boxes that apply to you. Have you ever . . .

- ❑ cheated on a test?
- ❑ taken something that wasn't yours?
- ❑ locked your little brother in a closet with only graham crackers and water (or maybe that's just me)?
- ❑ been ashamed of the way you represented God?

Most of us have done things that were not the best things to do. Sometimes we think that because of those things, God must be mad at us and therefore does not want to use us. This is not true. God uses even the most messed-up people to accomplish huge things for Him. Tell God that you're sorry for the times you have messed up—you can be specific—and that you are grateful that He still wants to use you.

3—WIMPS ALLOWED

Flip to Acts 7:55-59 today. Thank you!

Carl was wearing his WWJD bracelet when a group of people on the bus started throwing things at him and yelling, "What would Jesus do now?" Carl didn't know what to do so he tried to ignore them, but it only got worse. When he got off the bus, they chased him as he ran home. When he got home, he felt like he had failed God. He wanted to be strong and stand up to them, but instead he just ran and hid.

What do you think Carl should do now? Here's an idea: He can pray to God, asking God to help him be stronger next time. No one is perfect—we all wimp out at times (undoubtedly, even Stephen had his wimpy days). The goal is to learn from those times when we are wimps and pray even more that God will use us in the future.

When have you failed to share about God, even when you had the chance? What does that tell you about yourself? What would you like to tell God about what happened, and how you felt afterwards? How should that guide the way you pray right now?

4—REPRIORITIZE!

Friends, Romans and teens, lend me your ears. Oh, and look up Romans 12:1-2 to see what God wants you to hear.

What are some things that take up your time? (Check all that apply.)

❑	sports	❑	friends
❑	music	❑	phone/texting
❑	church	❑	Internet
❑	homework (yuck)	❑	reading
❑	TV/video games	❑	chores (double yuck)

All too often, other things take up our time and God loses out. It is easy to think that we are in too deep to get out of some patterns we have set. But God is always there for us when we want to change those habits. In fact, He will help us do so.

Just because you may have made God a low priority in the past doesn't mean that He loves you any less, or that you can't make changes today. Ask God to help you make Him a larger priority right now. Ask Him to use you as a bold witness! Be careful—you might just change the world.

LET'S EAT

THE BIG IDEA

Jesus has broken down every barrier that keeps us from Him and each other.

SESSION AIMS

In this session you will guide students to (1) understand the struggle of the Early Church to accept Gentiles as true believers; (2) realize the power of the gospel to break down the barriers that separate people from God and each other; and (3) experience the Holy Spirit at work in their own lives as a barrier breaker.

THE BIGGEST VERSE

"There is neither Jew nor Greek, slave nor free, male nor female, for you are all one in Christ Jesus" (Galatians 3:28).

OTHER IMPORTANT VERSES

Genesis 12:2-3; Matthew 5:21-28; John 17:23; Acts 1:8; 6; 7; 9–11; 1 Corinthians 12:12-14,27

Note: Additional options and worksheets in 8¹/₂" x 11" format for this session are available for download at **www.gospellight.com/uncommon/jh_the_new_testament.zip**.

STARTER

Option 1: Defying Expectations. For this option, you need three bottles of very different-flavored, but similar-colored, sodas (such as root beer, Dr. Pepper and Pepsi/Coke) and cups. Switch the contents of the bottles so that the labels and the contents don't match.

Greet students and ask them what they remember from the last two sessions. If all you get are blank stares, a few gentle reminders might help, such as the Day of Pentecost, the Holy Spirit, Peter, beggars leaping around, and other wild miracles. Explain that today, you'll be looking at a difficult time in the life of the Early Church—one in which they learned that things aren't always what they are expected to be.

Ask if anyone is thirsty. Choose three volunteers from the sea of raised hands and give each one a cup and a bottle of the mixed-up soda.

Let them drink as you continue to talk about today's lesson. There should be a halting "What *is* this?" along with quizzical looks at the bottle's label to see what you gave them to drink. Play along, pretending you don't understand what they are talking about—looking at the bottle, reading the label, and so on—but after a minute or two, confess that you switched the contents of the bottles to see if they would notice.

Now ask the volunteers the following questions:

- What did you expect to drink? (*Whatever the label on the bottle said.*)
- What happened when you took that first sip? (*I didn't get the flavor that I thought I would.*)

Discuss the following with the group:

- What are some other times when you have expected one thing but got another? (*Allow students to respond.*)
- Was it hard to change your expectations? (*The point to draw out is that it is always hard to change our expectations because it involves releasing control—something nobody likes to do!*)
- What religion was Jesus raised in? (*Judaism.*)
- Who were the first people to believe in Jesus? (*They were Jews.*)
- To whom did Peter preach on the day of Pentecost? (*Jews who were celebrating a Jewish feast in Jerusalem.*)
- What kind of people would those first believers expect to join their group? (*Jews like themselves.*)

- What kind of people were added to the Church? (*Jews and Gentiles, meaning non-Jews.*)
- Was this an easy transition? (*Let students begin to probe the idea, but you will be delving deeper into this issue in the next session.*)

Transition to the next step by stating that God often does things in unexpected ways. The Early Church, which was made up of Jews, had to move over and make room for the Gentiles, even though it was awkward and difficult at first. As we'll see, they had to learn that the gospel was meant for everyone.

Option 2: Everybody In. For this option, you need masking tape, a watch with a seconds indicator, and candy or other goodies for prizes. Use the masking tape to make three 2' x 2' squares on the floor, at least 8 feet apart.

Greet students and have them call out facts they remember from the last two sessions, awarding a prize for every pertinent fact or important concept they can remember. If all you get are blank stares, a few gentle reminders might help, such as the Day of Pentecost, the Holy Spirit, Peter, beggars leaping around, and other wild miracles. Explain that today you're going to continue looking at the book of Acts and the Early Church, but first you're going to play a game.

Divide students into three teams and explain that each team has one minute to get each of its team members inside the square marked on the floor. No part of anyone's body can be outside of the line—no toes, no fingers, no shoelaces . . . you get the point. Students can climb on each other's backs as long as it doesn't endanger anyone's safety. Signal to start and stop when the first team gets all its members into their square.

Award prizes to the winning team and have everyone sit down, and then discuss the following:

- Why was it hard to get everyone inside the square? (*It was a small space, we couldn't all fit.*)
- What would be the easiest solution? (*To say that some people couldn't be a part.*)
- Have you ever had to make room for someone you knew and liked? Was it easy? (*Yes, it is always easy to squeeze in someone you like.*)
- Have you ever had to make room for someone you didn't like? Was that easy? (*No, we are much less accommodating to people that we don't care about.*)

Explain that this is exactly like what happened to the Early Church. Jesus had been raised from the dead, the Holy Spirit had been given to the believers, and they were moving right along. Then it happened: God started saving the Gentiles—that is, non-Jews! This was completely awkward, uncomfortable and very unexpected (not to mention un-kosher—literally)! Today we're going to see how the Early Church learned that the gospel was meant for everyone.

MESSAGE

Option 1: Toe Fishing. For this option, you need several Bibles, a watch with a seconds indicator, a large cooler, cold water, a bunch of marbles, and candy or other goodies for prizes. Fill the cooler with cold water and add the marbles.

Begin by explaining that the central theme for the book of Acts is Acts 1:8. Read the verse, and then explain that so far we have focused primarily on how we are called to be witnesses of Jesus Christ, but today we're going to focus on to whom we're supposed to be witnesses. Reread the last part of Acts 1:8, emphasizing the words "Judea and Samaria, and to the ends of the earth."

Continue by stating that right from the start, Jesus said that His message was meant to be taken not just to the Jewish believers but also to the Gentile (non-Jewish) world as well. This is no news to us, but it was radical to the Early Church! They had been raised to think of only themselves as God's chosen people—because they were His chosen ones. The father of the Jewish people, Abraham, had received this promise from God: "I will make you a great nation and I will bless you; I will make your name great, and you will be a blessing. I will bless those who bless you, and whoever curses you I will curse; and all peoples on earth will be blessed through you" (Genesis 12:2-3). What the Jewish Christians didn't know yet is that Jesus' death was the fulfillment of that promise! God sent His Son, Jesus, to bless all people—Gentiles included—with the gift of salvation. Peter and the other Jewish believers learned in a dramatic way that the gospel wasn't just for the Jews, but for all who will come to Jesus.

Youth Leader Tip
Junior-highers love to talk. Invite them to share their ideas, and if they disagree with each other (or—*gasp, shudder*—with you), use the opportunity as training in critical thinking and reasoning.

Distribute Bibles and read Acts 10:1-48. (This is a long but story-like passage of Scripture, so you should be able to keep the students' interest as long as you put a little feeling into what you're reading.[1]) After reading the passage, divide students into two teams and instruct them to remove their shoes and socks and line up about 10 feet from the cooler. Explain that you'll be alternating teams, asking the first team member in line a question from the story you just read. He or she has 10 seconds to answer. If the correct answer is given, he or she will run to the cooler and place one foot in the water. He or she will have 10 seconds to fish out as many marbles as possible, one marble at a time—with his or her toes! Then it's the other team's turn. Ask a question, and if the person gets it right within 10 seconds, he or she can go toe fishing for 10 seconds.

If a team member cannot answer correctly, within the allotted time, the next person up on the other team gets to take a crack at the answer. The team with the most points (marbles) at the end of the game wins. (*Note:* Keep in mind that this game works best at a fast pace, keeping the students attentive and on their feet.) Here are the questions:

- What was Cornelius's job? (*He was a Roman centurion.*)
- What kind of person was he? (*A devout man who feared God.*)
- Was Cornelius a Jew or a Gentile? (*He was a Gentile.*)
- What happened as Cornelius was praying? (*An angel from God came and told him to go to Joppa and get Peter.*)
- What was Peter doing when Cornelius's messengers came to him? (*He was praying and saw a vision.*)
- Was Peter a Jew or a Gentile? (*He was a Jew.*)
- What did Peter see in the vision? (*A sheet full of unclean animals that God told him he could kill and eat. You may need to explain the concept of "unclean animals" to the group.*)
- What was Peter's response when he heard this? (*No! I've never eaten unclean food.*)
- How many times did Peter see this vision? (*Three times.*)
- Did Peter go with the messengers? (*Yes.*)
- What did Cornelius do when Peter arrived? (*He fell at Peter's feet.*)
- What did Peter do at Cornelius's home? (*He preached a sermon.*)
- What happened while Peter was preaching to Cornelius's household? (*The Holy Spirit came on the Gentile believers, just as He had done on the Day of Pentecost.*)
- What was Peter's reaction to this? (*He was amazed.*)

You can cycle through these questions a few times if necessary—the idea is that the students walk away with a full understanding of the story. After you award prizes to the winning team, explain that this story is important because it shows us that God's plan was that His message of salvation would reach into every nation and people group. The Early Church changed from "Jews only" to "everyone welcome."

Option 2: A Little Drama. For this option, you need some enthusiastic and dramatic kids. Before you present the main text, discuss the following questions as background:

- Why are the Jews so special? (*The Jews were chosen by God to enjoy a special relationship with God through the covenants, or promises, that He made with them—first with Abraham and then with the whole nation.*)

- What was the purpose of the Jewish laws? (*These laws helped the Jews remember that they were different from other people in the world. God had called them into a special relationship with Himself called a covenant; to break the law would be to step outside of the covenant. No devout Jew would even think about doing it.*)

Ask for volunteers to act out a melodrama. You need the following characters: Cornelius, an angel, two messengers, a soldier, Peter, some unclean animals (you may need to explain the concept to your students), the Holy Spirit and some of Peter's Christian brothers. The rest of the group can act as Cornelius's family and friends.

Read Acts 10:1-48 and invite the actors to stage their play. Pause as much as needed, and give direction as necessary. When the play is finished and the group gives themselves a round of applause, discuss the following questions:

- Why was Peter so shocked when he saw the vision? (*Because to eat unclean animals went against the Jewish dietary laws. It was a total reverse of everything he had been raised to obey as far as eating was concerned. It would be as repulsive to Peter as it would be to you if someone were to set a plate of human earlobes at your table and say, "Bon appetit!"*)

- Did God contradict Himself by telling Peter to eat the unclean animals and go to a Gentile's home? (*God sometimes does things that shock us.*

He never goes against His Word, but sometimes our preconceived ideas block God's plan. Just like Peter, we think we know exactly how God works and that we've got Him all figured out, but because of Jesus, there are new standards. In this case, God set aside the dietary laws for the Gentiles, just as He later set aside the laws for circumcision for them as well.)

- What was God trying to show Peter though this vision? (*That He had opened the message of salvation to all people, not just the Jews.*)

- What does this story teach us? (*No matter what color, what language, what custom—if they are truly His people, He desires them to love and accept each other and bring His message of love to the world.*)

- According to Acts 1:8, who are we to be witnesses to? (*To Jerusalem [our hometown], Judea and Samaria [the surrounding cities and states] and to the ends of the earth [every nation under the sun].*)

DIG

Option 1: No Outcasts Allowed. For this option, you need a watch with a seconds indicator and some adult volunteers. Announce that students have 15 seconds to form groups of three. This should immediately exclude at least one or two students, so have the adult volunteers ready to jump in and form groups with those who are left. Discuss the following:

- Why did you group up with those particular people? (*They are my friends; I wanted to be with someone I like.*)
- How would you feel if I regrouped you? (*No! I want to stay with my friends!*)
- What would you feel if everyone grouped up and left you out? (*Hurt, alone, mad.*)
- What makes someone an outcast? (*People overlook them or deliberately choose not to include them for some reason.*)
- Think about kids at your school whom no one likes. What is it about them that makes them an outcast? (*Allow students to share general characteristics or labels, but not names.*)
- How are they treated? (*They are excluded, made fun of, talked down to, and so forth.*)

- Do they deserve to be treated that way? (*Maybe, or maybe not. Allow the students to share their opinions, but keep the talk focused on being exclusive.*)

Next, ask a volunteer to read 1 John 4:19-21, and then continue the discussion. (*Note:* The last two questions might be better as silent challenges rather than group discussions):

- Where does the ability to love come from? (*From God; He loved us first.*)
- Do we deserve God's love? (*No.*)
- What does this passage say about loving God? (*That if we love God, we must love others as well.*)
- In what ways have you been excluding others just because you didn't really like them?
- What can you do to include them?

Conclude by stating that while others may or may not deserve to be loved and accepted, neither did we. As Christians, God wants us to show the same kindness and love to others as He has to us. This doesn't mean you have to be best friends with everyone you come in contact with, but it does mean that you should never exclude someone on purpose. The Church is made up of all kinds of people, but the common bond we share is that we are part of one big family—God's.

Option 2: Different Strokes. For this option, you need just this book!
Share the following case study:

Kyle and Suzanne belonged to different churches. Both congregations were committed to the Bible as the Word of God and both agreed on all the basic teachings of the Christian faith, but Suzanne grew up in a charismatic church. She was used to clapping and moving around during worship, passionate sermons and congregational hallelujahs and amens that popped up from time to time. Her friend Kyle, however, was from a traditional church that worshiped in a more structured and liturgical style.

When Suzanne was invited to visit Kyle's youth group, she was not prepared for the differences. The next day, she made fun of Kyle's church to her friends—the music, the message and the slower, low-key pace of the service. Just as she was doing a full-on impression of the youth pastor, Kyle walked up. Suzanne tried to smooth things over, but it was too late. Kyle was hurt and angrily walked away.

Now discuss the following questions:

- Have you ever visited a church that worshiped differently from what you were used to? (*Allow for responses and examples, but don't let anyone use the differences as a springboard for gossip.*)
- Is there only one way to have a church service? (*No, there is no formula. How a service is run is far less important than what is being taught.*)
- What was Suzanne's first mistake? (*She compared Kyle's church with her own; instead of enjoying the differences, she criticized Kyle's church.*)
- What was Suzanne's second mistake? (*She took her criticism and spread it around at school.*)
- What was Kyle's mistake? (*Instead of being angry, he could have extended forgiveness to Suzanne, and maybe even offered to visit her church so they could talk about the two styles afterward.*)
- Can churches worship differently but still be worshiping Jesus? (*Sure! We have to learn to distinguish between style and belief.*)
- What is the most important thing to consider about a church? (*Whether or not the Bible basics are being taught as truth. Church is more about non-negotiable beliefs than negotiable traditions.*)
- What if you go to a church and the Bible is not the foundation for their beliefs? (*Skedaddle out of there as soon as you can, but remember to still respect the people, even though you don't accept the beliefs.*)

APPLY

Option 1: I Am Not Alone. For this option, you need a window with the glass pane still in it, the song "I Am Not Alone" from Natalie Grant's self-titled album (download the song or pick up a copy of the CD), a way to play the song, and several adult volunteers. Ahead of time, prepare adult volunteers to pray with students.

Hold up the window. Explain to the group that windows allow us to look in places we normally couldn't. They keep out bad weather and bugs, and that's good! But windows can also remind us of the unacceptance we feel at times—especially when it comes to having a living relationship with Jesus. Maybe you have always felt like the odd man (or woman) out at church—the one who has never really been accepted. You look through the window of Christianity and see other people having good relationships with each other and God, but you have never really experienced that yourself. Today I want you to know—without a doubt—that God loves and accepts you. You can spend your whole life going to church and feel like you're on the outside of the window looking in, or you can change it by opening the door to a personal relationship with God. Jesus has opened that window, and He stands ready to welcome you if you will simply come in.

Play "I Am Not Alone" as students have a time of quiet reflection. (*Note:* After playing the song, consider reading the lyrics aloud to make sure students really understand the message.) Ask those who would like to be prayed with—either to ask Jesus to take over their lives or for something else—to come forward. Have adult volunteers ready to pray and instruct the rest of the group to continue worshiping with the music. End with corporate prayer, thanking God for His incredible gift of love and acceptance in Jesus.

Option 2: Practicing Unity. For this option, you need a plan, Stan. Oh! Paper and a pen or pencil for your notes. Ahead of time, arrange a time for students to serve another youth group (especially one from a different tradition or ethnicity) by hosting an event such as a pizza dinner, a worship concert, a game night—anything to show friendship and unity. It's best if you have selected a group and a date so that your students can plan the specifics of the event.

Begin by explaining that just like Peter and the Early Church, we need to accept others who have a genuine relationship with Jesus, even if they don't attend our church or keep our church traditions. As we learn in John 17:23, by showing acceptance and love, we are demonstrating how God welcomes and receives His children.

Explain that the group has an opportunity to put this into practice this very minute—you will all be serving (insert the other youth group and the date here). Now all you have to do is figure out what to do! Allow plenty of time for students to brainstorm ideas for serving the visiting youth group and then choose the actual activity through a vote. Divide up the responsibilities so that every student can contribute something. Create a list of students and their assigned responsibilities, and then be sure to check in with them as the date approaches.

Close in prayer, asking God to use this event to bring a greater unity in the Body of Christ.

REFLECT

The following short devotions are for the students to reflect on and answer during the week. You can make a copy of these pages and distribute to your class or download and print from **www.gospellight.com/uncommon/jh_ the_new_testament.zip.**

1—LOVE YOUR ENEMIES

You must go to Matthew 5:43-45.
   Do you know someone who (check all that apply):

❑   is a bully at your school?
❑   has a bad attitude toward teachers?
❑   has been in a physical fight?
❑   makes you really mad?

Jesus says that we are supposed to love our enemies. That seems so weird. In our world, you avoid your enemies, even try to get revenge against them, but you certainly don't *love* them! *Why* would Jesus say this?
   Jesus came to teach us how God wants us to live. By loving your enemies you ultimately love God. Think of some people who are hard for you to love. Tell God you want to love Him today by loving these people. Ask Him for His strength, as it will no doubt be hard—actually impossible—without His power.

2—ACCEPT, NOT EXCEPT

Be careful—Romans 15:7 just might make you think!
   Gwen was pretty popular at school and she and her friends all seemed to belong to the "in" crowd. There was a new girl at school named Megan. Megan had glasses and jeans that had holes in them. At Megan's old school she was teased all the time. To Megan's surprise, Gwen invited her to eat lunch with her and her friends. Megan was blown away at Gwen's kindness.
   The story rarely turns out like this. So many times we judge other people and don't accept them at all. God clearly says in Romans 15:7 that He wants us to accept other people for two reasons: (1) We need to accept others because God accepts us; and (2) when we accept others, we bring praise to God.
   Do you want to bring praise to God? Try to be accepting of other people. Who can you invite to eat lunch with you and your friends today?

3—LET THE ANGER GO

Do five jumping jacks and turn to James 1:19-20.
What really gets you angry? Check all that apply:

- ❑ When someone eats all of the dessert before you get any (Maybe you should have finished off those green beans a little quicker.)
- ❑ When you have a substitute teacher who actually makes you do schoolwork
- ❑ When your little sister bugs you while you are on the phone or on-line with that special someone
- ❑ When you have a bad game

So many times we get angry with other people. This anger can really hinder how we relate to each other. As followers of Christ, we should be able to look past the anger because God looks past all of the stuff that we do. When we really experience God in our lives, we realize that anger is not cool in God's eyes.

Who are you angry at today? How can you look past the feeling of anger you might have toward that person? Go ahead; try it!

4—WHEN TO FORGIVE?

Colossians 3:13 is calling your name.

Tim and Nathan have been friends for a really long time. Last week, Tim got really upset because Nathan accidentally broke one of his video games. Nathan felt so bad about breaking the game that he borrowed money from his parents to replace it. The next day, Nathan took the new game and went over to Tim's house. He asked Tim to forgive him for breaking the game and handed him the new one. Tim forgave Nathan and they went inside to play the new game.

Should Tim have forgiven Nathan even if he hadn't replaced the game? Look at Colossians 3:13 again. So many times we don't forgive people who have hurt us, whether they ask for forgiveness or not.

Who are some people who you might need to forgive? Pray for them by name today and ask God what He might want you to do.

FROM KILLER TO CRUSADER

THE BIG IDEA

God's power can set our life course in the right direction and give us the power to share His message with others.

SESSION AIMS

In this session you will guide students to (1) realize that God has a sovereign plan for their lives that involves sharing His message with others; (2) feel encouraged that the power to accomplish that plan lies in God's strong grace; and (3) rejoice in God's ability to use them to impact the world for Christ this week.

THE BIGGEST VERSE

"At once [Paul] began to preach in the synagogues that Jesus is the Son of God. All those who heard him were astonished and asked, 'Isn't he the man who raised havoc in Jerusalem among those who call on this name?'" (Acts 9:20-21).

OTHER IMPORTANT VERSES

Acts 1:8; 7:58; 9:1-22; 11:26; 19:23; 22:3,12; 1 Corinthians 1:26-29; 15:1-8; Galatians 1:14

Note: Additional options and worksheets in 8¹/₂" x 11" format for this session are available for download at **www.gospellight.com/uncommon/jh_the_new_testament.zip**.

STARTER

Option 1: Believers and Unbelievers. You will need a space with lots of hiding places, such as a playground or park. Determine boundaries for this modified game of hide and seek. Also, designate a place to be a jail for captured players.

Greet students and state that we've learned through getting to know Peter that the Church's job is to continue to take God's message to the world around us through the power of the Holy Spirit. Explain that today you're going to learn about another famous apostle who went from being a killer of Christians to a crusader for the truth.

Divide students into two equal teams: Believers and Unbelievers. Give the Believers two minutes to find hiding places within the prearranged boundaries (Unbelievers should cover their eyes—no peeking!). The Unbelievers will then try to find the Believers and arrest them by walking them over to jail. Here's the twist: The Believers can share the gospel with the Unbelievers, giving the Unbeliever a chance to accept Christ and join their side, hiding with them instead of dragging them to jail. An Unbeliever should only choose to join the side of the Believers if the person they've tagged gives a very convincing explanation of the gospel or why he or she is a Believer. The game continues until all the Believers are found or all the Unbelievers have changed sides by accepting Christ (or everyone is getting tired of playing).

Regroup and explain that, oftentimes, people who are on one side of something go through a radical change and begin to support the very thing they attacked. Just like in our game, some of the Unbelievers responded to the gospel message and switched sides to become a part of the Believers. Today we're going to see how God brought a very unlikely person from attacking the Church to strengthening it.

Option 2: Opposites. For this option, you need nothing but this study!

Greet students and ask them to tell you three things they remember from the previous sessions. Explain that you're going to play an opposite association game. Have the group form a circle and sit on the ground. Begin a rhythm by slapping your knees twice and then clapping twice. When you clap, call out a word that has an obvious opposite (for example, light/dark, wet/dry, tall/short, and so on). Beginning on your right, go around the circle and have students respond by calling back the first opposite that comes to mind. You call a word, then one by one students answer you back.

Continue calling out words until everyone in the circle has had an opportunity to respond. At the conclusion of the game, discuss the following:

- Can someone go from truly hating something to truly liking it? (*Allow for responses.*)

- What are some examples of this that you've seen or heard? (*Examples could involve food items, music, clothes, people, and so forth.*)

- Have you ever experienced going from one opinion about something to the exact opposite opinion? (*Allow for responses and be prepared with a personal story to share.*)

- What happened that changed your mind? (*Help students realize that there is usually a definite, deciding moment that initiates a big change.*)

Explain that today you're going to continue to study the book of Acts and learn about a man who went the complete opposite direction from where he started. He was a strong opponent of the Early Church's message—even to the point of murdering Christians—but after his own radical encounter with Jesus, he became a defender of the very gospel he had attacked.

MESSAGE

Option 1: Acts 9:1-22 Mural. For this option, you need your Bible, a hat, 22 small pieces of paper, a long sheet of newsprint (or butcher paper), felt-tip pens and masking tape. Number the small pieces of paper from 1 to 22, fold them and put them in the hat, and then tape the newsprint across a wall and write the numbers 1 to 22 across the top, leaving space between each number for students to draw pictures.

Begin by explaining how amazing it is the way a personal experience with Jesus can change your life. A person can be heading one way and then, through the power of God, be completely changed and set on another path going in a completely different direction. Paul experienced this in a dramatic way. Today, the group is going to help you tell his story in Acts 9:1-22.

Youth Leader Tip
Use maps to locate specific cities or regions mentioned in passages you are studying.[1] Doing this helps students grasp where the events took place and that the places they are reading about are real!

One at a time, have students draw a number out of the hat. Instruct each student to look up the verse, read it and draw a picture in 20 seconds of what is described in their passage under the number that corresponds to their assigned verse (yes, given only 20 seconds, some of the students will have pretty bad drawings, but that's part of the fun). Remind students to draw under their assigned number or the story will be out of order! When everyone is finished, have them return to their seats and ask a volunteer to read Acts 9:1-22 (the rest of the group can follow along by looking at the mural).

Explain that Paul was a Pharisee, a zealous defender of Jewish law. He felt that the Jesus followers were a threat to Judaism and sought to stop them—by killing them if necessary.[2] But when he encountered Jesus Christ on that road to Damascus, his life did a complete U-turn. He went from being a persecutor to a defender of the gospel message. It was so radical that the Jews and believers were wondering if it was the same man! They couldn't grasp how someone could change so radically. But he did change! He met Jesus. And, just like Paul, the power of God can change our lives and put us on the right path as well.

Option 2: Paul of Tarsus. For this option, you need several Bibles, copies of "Paul of Tarsus" (found on the next page), a compass, a pair of dark sunglasses and a microphone.

Read Acts 9:1-2, and then explain that before we can understand why Paul was an unlikely person to tell the Gentiles about Jesus, we have to understand a little bit about his background. Distribute "Paul of Tarsus" and ask a volunteer to read through the highlighted facts about Paul. Explain that because of Paul's enthusiasm for the Jewish faith and his deep training in Jewish law, he opposed everything that he believed threatened Judaism—including the followers of Jesus. Paul felt that the believers were blaspheming God because they worshiped Jesus too.

Ask the group members, "What do you do when you think you've learned everything you possibly can, but you're missing one key point?" Show the compass and explain that if a person were charting a course but wasn't careful in his or her measurements, the person might get started just one or two degrees off. That misdirection would be no big deal at first, but given enough time and distance, the person would soon wind up way off course. That's what happened with Paul. He got so caught up in the Jewish laws that He forgot what they were for: to give him the chance to know God. His course was off just a few degrees, and over time it had taken him so far away from the right path that he couldn't recognize Jesus as the Messiah.

 # PAUL OF TARSUS

- Born in Tarsus, which is located in modern-day Turkey on the Mediterranean Sea. Although this was not really a Jewish city, it had a significant Jewish community, of which Paul's family was a part (see Acts 22:3).

- Grew up in a very Jewish home; his dad was a Pharisee—an educated and dedicated student of the Jewish laws (see Acts 23:6).

- Was taught by Gamaliel, the chief leader of the Pharisees in Jerusalem (see Philippians 3:5).

- Zealous for the Jewish faith and highly committed to its teachings (see Galatians 1:14).

- Held the coats of the men who stoned Stephen, the first Christian martyr (see Acts 7:58).

- Had warrants for the arrest and imprisonment of the believers (see Acts 9:1-2).

Continue by stating that there were three things that happened to correct Paul's course. First, he encountered Jesus personally. When Jesus reveals Himself to us personally, we realize our deep need for Him and are humbled. Read Acts 9:3-9 and explain that God had a plan for Paul, and that plan included sharing the message of Jesus Christ with others. Even though Paul was the complete opposite of a Gentile, God had chosen him to be an apostle to the Gentiles. He began to preach the very message he had opposed at one time to the very people he had despised!

Point out the progression to the students: Paul saw a bright light, fell to the ground, heard a voice and became a changed man—blind, but obedient. Put on the sunglasses, and ask the group, "Why did Paul become blind? Why not deaf? Why not mute?" Explain that it was because *seeing* was the very area in which he needed to be changed. When Jesus came to him, the truth was revealed and Paul was able to realize his dilemma: he couldn't really see *anything*. He needed a brand-new perspective.

Continue by stating that the second thing that happened to correct Paul's course was that he allowed others to help. In the same way, we need to accept the instruction of wiser, respected leaders. Read Acts 9:10-19 and discuss how Ananias was a believer and well respected by the Jews (see 22:12). God instructed Ananias to go to Paul and pray for him. This wasn't an easy thing for Ananias because of Paul's reputation as a fierce opponent of the Early Church. And it wasn't easy for Paul who, until now, had probably never even entered a Gentile's home, let alone accepted spiritual help from one.

Ask a volunteer to come up and remove your sunglasses. Explain that this shows us that we need the God-inspired help of other mature believers— friends, parents, youth pastors or other leaders—to help get us on track with God's plan for our lives. God will use others to release us into our calling.

Continue by stating that the third thing that happened to Paul to correct his course was that he responded with obedience to what God had said. Likewise, we need to do what God has put in our hearts to do. Read Acts 9:20-22 and explain that without hesitation, Paul began to witness to others about the power of Jesus Christ to forgive sins and change hearts. He testified about his own experience. Hold up the microphone as a symbol for telling others about Jesus. Explain that this is the result of a personal encounter with Jesus: we are truly changed and can't help but tell others.

Conclude by stating that this is not to say that everything will be perfect or that life will be one wonderful event after another—things heated up pretty quickly for Paul after his conversion, as can happen for all of Jesus' followers.

However, God has promised to stand with us through good and bad! With Him we are never lost. Just like Paul, our lives can be set in the right direction when we personally encounter Jesus Christ and let His power change our lives.

DIG

Option 1: Step Up to the Microphone. For this option, you need a microphone, the title song off the Newsboys album *Step Up to the Microphone* (download the song or pick up a copy of the CD), and a way to play the song.

Begin by stating that just like Paul, when we've experienced God's power in our lives, we can't help but show it in our attitude, words and actions. Ask the group to listen to the words of the song (you might also want to print out the lyrics). After you play the title song, discuss the following:

- What is the message of this song? (*Sharing the gospel with others.*)
- Why is it important that we tell others what God has done for us? (*All believers are called to continue to share the message of God's forgiveness.*)
- How would you briefly explain the gospel message? (*Discuss the core of the gospel, including these basic truths: The Son of God came as a man to offer His life to save all people; He died, was buried and rose on the third day. Now we have to respond to Him and decide whether to ask Him to control our lives and be our Savior and Lord, or not. You might want to use your church's statement of faith as a resource for summarizing the basic truths of the gospel.*)

Read 1 Corinthians 15:1-8. Explain that Paul wrote this to the first believers at Corinth to remind them of the power that had changed their lives—the power given by Jesus through His Holy Spirit. Paul knew this power personally because he had experienced it on the road to Damascus. He was a different man, and everyone could tell.

Youth Leader Tip
When is the best time to stop an activity? When everyone is tired of it? Actually, the best time is just *before* they all get tired of it. That way, they will look forward to experiencing it another time.

Pass the microphone around and give students the opportunity to share one way that God has touched their lives. Encourage them to think of times when God redirected their course and set them on the right path—whether that was their initial salvation experience or a time when they stood up against peer pressure—and also how the changes in them encouraged others to put their faith in Christ.

Option 2: Unlikely World-Changer. For this option, you need the following short biography. Share the first part of the following real-life case study:

He didn't talk until the age of three. He hated the dull routine and unimaginative talk of school and failed his elementary math class. When he was 15 years old, he dropped out of school altogether. Later, when he tried to finish his education, he cut classes to play his violin. He passed his examinations and graduated only by studying the notes of a classmate. His professors did not think highly of him and refused to recommend him for a job.

Now discuss the following:

- What kind of potential would you think this person has to impact the world? (*Not much!*)
- How can you tell whether or not someone has the ability to change the world? (*You can't always tell. But God knows, and He has a perfect plan to use every single person to help spread His message to others.*)

Now share the second part of the case study:

This man became an internationally renowned physicist. His theories completely changed the way we view this world. He earned many honors and awards, including the Nobel Prize in physics in 1921. He was so famous that a visit to any part of the world became a national event; photographers and reporters followed him everywhere. Our whole world is different because of what this person did. What was his name? Albert Einstein!

Discuss the following:

- God often uses unlikely people to do great things. Can you think of another example of someone who did something that no one else thought possible? (*Allow for a few responses.*)

- What do these achievements tell us about how God can use us to impact the world? (*No matter how unlikely it may seem, God can—and will—use us to reach others for Christ.*)

APPLY

Option 1: Which Way Should I Go? For this option, you need copies of "Which Way Should I Go?" (found on the next page) and pens or pencils.

Begin by explaining that like Peter and Paul, we all have times when things need to be changed—radically changed—in our lives. At other times, we just need some minor adjustments; we're heading in the right direction, but could use a little of God's help to make sure we stay on track. And sometimes (these are the rarest ones) we feel like we're headed in exactly the direction God wants for us.

Distribute "Which Way Should I Go?" and pens or pencils and instruct students to complete each of the boxes as directed. Allow a few minutes for students to complete their handouts, and then explain that if we truly desire to be aligned with God's plan for our lives, we need to be totally honest with Him about the differences between what we think He wants for us and what *we* want. We need to ask for His help in following His will instead of our own.

Allow for a few moments of silent prayer, encouraging students to approach God with areas in which they are struggling to follow His will. Close in prayer, thanking God for His direction for our lives and asking Him to guide students as they seek His will.

Option 2: Used Up. For this option, you need copies of "Used Up" (found on page 161) and pens or pencils.

Explain that you're going to have a time of quiet reflection so that students can really think about God's plan for their lives. Tell the students that they aren't here in this place at this time by accident—God knew exactly when they would be born. Nothing about them is accidental, and He wants to bless them and use them to extend His message to others.

Review some of the notes about Paul's life, and then continue by stating that just as there were some special parts of Paul's background that helped contribute to God's plan for him, so the same is true for us.

Distribute "Used Up" and pens or pencils and ask students to consider some of their skills and any spiritual gifts they think they might have. Instruct them to write those things down on their handouts and to consider how God

WHICH WAY SHOULD I GO?

From the starting point, finish the path (dotted line) in Box One by drawing a line indicating the direction you think that God wants you to go (toward the cross). For example, if you are currently going in the complete opposite of where you think God wants you, draw a U-turn; if you think you're okay but need some corrective driving, draw a couple of turns . . . and so on.

BOX ONE

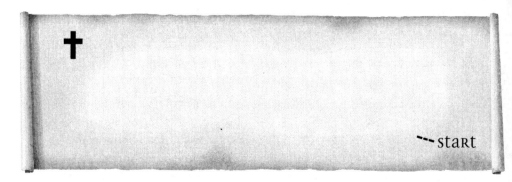

Now finish the path in Box Two by showing where you *want* to be headed.

BOX TWO

USED UP

Just like Paul, God has given you some amazing experiences that will become part of how He wants to use you to impact others around you.

Four things I've experienced:	These four experiences could be used by God in these ways:
1.	
2.	
3.	
4.	

If I let God change the following two things about me, I might be more ready to be used by Him:

1. _____
   _____
   _____

2. _____
   _____
   _____

might be able to use them and their unique talents and gifts to impact others in their lives. Conclude by praying for students that God would give them His grace to change direction where needed for them to become fervent followers of Jesus Christ—following His plan, His power and His timing.

REFLECT

The following short devotions are for the students to reflect on and answer during the week. You can make a copy of these pages and distribute to your class or download and print from **www.gospellight.com/uncommon/jh_ the_new_testament.zip.**

1—SCARY!

Go get a glass of milk and then turn to Matthew 28:19-20.
   Rank these in order (1 to 5) of what is the scariest for you:

_____   Being home alone at night
_____   Telling your friends about Jesus
_____   Inviting friends to church
_____   Getting a sloppy kiss from your Aunt Kimmy
_____   Finding out there is no Cinnamon Toast Crunch left

   Jesus tells us to go and make disciples of all nations. That means that God wants us to tell everyone about Jesus. Sometimes this seems so scary, but remember—the *same* power that raised Jesus from the dead is the power that God gives to share His message. God wants you to spend your life telling people about Him.
   How does that make you feel? Tell God how you feel right now about sharing the gospel, even if you're a little scared!

2—NEVER SAY NEVER

Read Romans 15:16, whether you're a Jew or a Gentile.
   Ruben has been praying for his friend Gil for a few years. Sometimes Ruben thinks that Gil will never accept Jesus. Gil has heard about Christianity and chosen not to believe in it. Ruben has chosen to live in a way that is consistent with following God, which includes trying not to cuss anymore. He's also made a commitment to keep praying for Gil every single day until Gil asks Jesus to take over his life too.
   Do you know someone who has made a decision *not* to follow Jesus? Remember: Praying for that person leaves room for God to answer your prayer.

God wants us to tap into His power and pray for people we think might not ever come to know Jesus as their Savior. In fact, why don't you try it right now?

3—LOST

Have you ever read Matthew 9:35-38? Get there and find out.

If you lost these things, would you care or not?

☐ Yes	☐ No	A shiny nickel
☐ Yes	☐ No	A can of soda
☐ Yes	☐ No	A pet
☐ Yes	☐ No	A report card
☐ Yes	☐ No	A note from someone you have a crush on

When we lose things, we might feel bad or even sad. In Matthew 9:36, the Bible describes how Jesus feels about people who are lost.

God desires to have all of His children call Him Lord. What is your responsibility in that? Pray for five people you know who are like the lost sheep. Ask God to help you know how to love them and share about Him this week.

4—THE GREATEST PARTY OF ALL TIME

Go find a quiet place (even if it's the bathroom!) and read Ephesians 1:7-10.

Earl's mom and Janet's dad got married several years ago. Earl and Janet planned their parents' surprise fifth-anniversary party. They sent out invitations, figured out the menu, had friends bring food and did all this in secret so their parents wouldn't find out.

When the day arrived, everything was perfect (except the cake, which was lopsided). Earl and Janet were glad they had worked so hard and invited so many people to such a great party. Everyone had a good time—and, best of all, their parents loved it!

God is going to have a big party—an eternity party—and He wants everyone to attend. Our job is to invite people to go. It's going to be hard work, but God wants to help us. He has given us the tools and the power to make the party as big as possible. Think of one person you would invite and pray for him or her right now!

OUT OF THE FRYING PAN AND INTO THE FIRE

THE BIG IDEA
God confirms His Word if we are faithful to preach it.

SESSION AIMS
In this session you will guide students to (1) grow in their understanding of how important it is to step out in faith; (2) feel encouraged to believe that God will confirm His Word; and (3) step out in obedience to God's Word this week.

THE BIGGEST VERSE
"So Paul and Barnabas spent considerable time there, speaking boldly for the Lord, who confirmed the message of his grace by enabling them to do miraculous signs and wonders" (Acts 14:3).

OTHER IMPORTANT VERSES
Matthew 12:28; Acts 1:3-8; 13:2-12; 14:8-10; 1 Corinthians 2:1-4; 2 Corinthians 4:4; Hebrews 4:12; 13:8

Note: Additional options and worksheets in 8^1/$_2$" x 11" format for this session are available for download at **www.gospellight.com/uncommon/jh_the_new_testament.zip**.

STARTER

Option 1: Way Maker. For this option, you need your Bible, sample carpet squares (you can get these from a carpet store or make your own with an old piece of carpet), candy or other goodies for prizes, and masking tape. Use the tape to mark start and finish lines for a race across the room.

Greet students and toss a prize to anyone who can tell you three facts about the apostle Paul that they remember from the last session. Explain that, so far, we've been studying the Early Church's effort to spread God's message and have seen that God often uses unlikely people to do this. Today, we are going to look at God's part in the process: He will confirm His Word when we are faithful to preach it.

Divide students into teams of three and give each team three carpet squares. Have each team choose one member as the Walker—the remaining two will be the Way Makers. The object of the game is to be the first Walker to get across the room, walking only on the carpet squares. The Way Makers will use the carpet squares to create a path, moving them one in front of the other as they're walked on to keep the path going.

After a winner has been declared, prizes have been awarded and everyone is seated, explain that this game illustrates exactly what God does for us as we step out to obey His Word: He goes before us and places our feet on the right path. When we are faithful to step out, God is faithful to support us and to confirm His Word.

Read Acts 14:3 and sum up by stating that Paul experienced God's confirmation of his ministry. God confirmed His Word in many dramatic ways when Paul spoke it. We're going to look at a few of those ways in this session.

Option 2: Climbing the Rock. For this option, you need your Bible and pictures of people mountain climbing and rappelling (check out sports magazines). (*Sports-nut option:* Bring in some climbing/rappelling gear—shoes, rope, clips and the like—to pass around during the discussion.)

Greet students and ask them to relate two facts about Peter and two facts about Paul based on the prior sessions. Begin this session by showing them the mountain climbers and rappellers, and then discuss the following:

- How would you feel about climbing the side of a steep mountain? (*Does it include a jetpack in case I fall?*)
- What outward difficulties might you encounter? (*Slippery footing, no footing, heat, wind, obstacles.*)

- What inward difficulties might you encounter? (*Fear of heights, lack of physical strength, and so forth.*)
- How could you overcome these obstacles? (*Train and plan ahead, get the right supplies, learn what you can about the technique and just do it— one step at a time!*)

Explain that God has given the Church the job of carrying on His message, but stepping out to obey God's Word and share the gospel with others can be a lot like climbing a mountain—there are many outward and inward struggles that can hinder us. Unlike the climbers, though, when we step out, our Rock— Jesus Christ—will support us by confirming His message.

Read Acts 14:3. Sum up by stating that Paul experienced God's confirmation in his ministry in many dramatic ways. Today, we're going to look at a few of those ways during this session.

MESSAGE

Option 1: Eyewitness Confirmation. For this option, you need several Bibles and four adult volunteers. Assign each volunteer one of the following Bible passages and characters: Acts 13:4-12—the Proconsul; Acts 14:8-10—the crippled man; Acts 16:11-15—Lydia; Acts 17:1-9—Jason. Ask them to prepare a short, detailed eyewitness testimony about the event. As an option, check with the children's ministry to see if there are any costumes the volunteers can use. (*Note:* You will be asking students detailed questions about each passage, so make sure the volunteers do a thorough job! You might want to pass on the questions you'll be asking so that the volunteers know what information to include.)

Ask for a show of hands to the following question: "How many of you remember watching the Disney movie *Cinderella*?" Next, ask the group if they remember the very end of the movie, when the stepmother trips the Prince's attendant and the glass slipper is broken. How did Cinderella still prove that she was the one the Prince danced with at the ball? (*She pulled the other slipper out of her pocket.*) Continue by explaining that the fact that Cinderella had the other slipper proved that she really was the one the Prince was looking for. That shoe added proof to who she really was. To "confirm" something is to add supporting proof to show that it is true. In a much more powerful way than glass slippers, God confirmed His Word when Paul was faithful to share it.

Read Acts 14:3 and explain that God confirmed His Word by doing many miraculous signs and wonders. Today, we're going to look at four different events and see four different ways that God proved His Word was true.

One at a time, have the volunteers share their eyewitness accounts from the Bible passage. After each account, use the following passage questions to discuss the event:

The Amazed Proconsul (Acts 13:4-12)
- Who sent Paul and Barnabas on their way? (*The Holy Spirit.*)
- Where did they sail to? (*The island of Cyprus.*)
- What did they do when they arrived at the city of Salamis? (*They proclaimed God's Word.*)
- Who came as their helper? (*John.*)
- Who did they meet when they arrived at the city of Paphos? (*A Jewish sorcerer and false prophet named Bar-Jesus.*)
- What was his job? (*Attendant to the proconsul—the Roman ruler there.*)
- What was the proconsul's name? (*Sergius Paulus.*)
- Why did the proconsul send for Paul and Barnabas? (*He wanted to hear the Word of God.*)
- What did the sorcerer do when they came to speak? (*He opposed Paul and Barnabas and tried to turn the proconsul against their message.*)
- What was Paul's reaction? (*He rebuked him and said he would be blind.*)
- What was the proconsul's reaction? (*He believed the message.*)

The Healing of the Crippled Man (Acts 14:8-10)
- What city was Paul in? (*Lystra.*)
- How long had the man been crippled? (*From birth.*)
- What was the crippled man doing? (*Listening to Paul share about Jesus.*)
- What did Paul see in the man when he looked at him? (*Faith.*)
- What did Paul say to the man? (*"Stand up."*)
- What happened to the man? (*He was healed.*)

A Gentile Woman Is Saved (Acts 16:11-15)
- What was Philippi? (*A Roman colony and the leading city of Macedonia.*)
- Where did Paul go on the Sabbath? (*Outside the city gate to the river.*)
- What was he looking for? (*A place to pray.*)
- What did he find? (*A group of women gathered at the river.*)
- Who was Lydia? (*A Gentile businesswoman from the city of Thyatira.*)
- Who opened her heart to Paul's words? (*God.*)
- What happened as a result? (*She and her household became believers and were baptized.*)

Arrest, Rejection and Persecution (Acts 17:1-9)

- At what city did Paul arrive? (*Thessalonica.*)
- What was Paul's custom when he entered a new city? (*To go to the synagogue and share the gospel.*)
- Who were the first to join Paul and believe his message? (*Some Jews, some God-fearing Greeks and some women.*)
- Who did not believe? (*Other Jews who were jealous of Paul.*)
- What did these jealous Jews do? (*Got a mob together to cause a riot.*)
- Where did the mob go to find Paul? (*Jason's house.*)
- What happened when they got there? (*They couldn't find Paul, so they arrested Jason and took him to the city officials.*)
- What was the accusation against Jason and the other believers? (*They were causing trouble all over the world.*)
- What was the officials' response? (*They became very upset.*)
- What happened to Jason? (*He posted bail and was released.*)

Pull all the passages together by discussing the following:

- In what different ways did God confirm His Word? (*In Cyprus, it was confirmed by a clear demonstration of the power and authority of God over the power of the darkness; in Lystra, it was confirmed by a miraculous healing; in Philippi, it was confirmed by the salvation of an entire household; and in Thessalonica, it was confirmed by rejection and persecution.*
- What pattern do we see in these examples? (*That when Paul was faithful to preach the gospel message, God confirmed His Word.*)
- How can persecution be considered a confirmation of God's Word? (*Because it is a valid response to His message. Jesus said that many would stumble because of His words; many would find them hard to believe. Rejection or persecution can be considered a sign that His truth is pricking the conscience of unbelievers, and in their rebellion, they act with hate and fear instead of love and surrender.*)
- Why do you think God confirmed His Word in different ways? Why didn't He do the same thing all the time? (*God knows what we need and works to accomplish His will, not ours. Sometimes we understand what He does and other times we don't. One thing we do know is that God has a perfect plan and our job is to obediently follow His direction. The results are up to Him. Paul was faithful to preach it, and he trusted God to draw the people to Himself—see 1 Corinthians 2:1-4.*)

Sum up by stating that when Paul was faithful to preach the Word, God was faithful to confirm it. We can believe that God will do the same for us too. As we are faithful to share what we know to be true, God will support us and prove His Word is true.[1]

Option 2: Confirmation Journeys. You will need your Bible, four volunteers and some masking tape. Use the tape to draw an outline of the four places Paul visited (Cyprus, Lystra, Philippi and Thessalonica) on the floor of the meeting room (the bigger the outline, the better). Also, ask the volunteers to act out the part of the main character who interacts with Paul in each place. You will play the part of Paul, journeying to each place and interacting with the characters.

Explain that a few weeks ago, we talked about how Jesus' miracles weren't done just to show off His power. Those miracles revealed God's glory, and when people saw the awesomeness of God, they put their trust in Him (see John 2:11). We also talked about how Jesus' miracles showed that God's kingdom was pushing out the kingdom of darkness (see Matthew 12:28).

When Jesus went back to heaven, He gave the Church the job of carrying on His message (see Acts 1:3-8). God's kingdom was to be extended through His followers. And this is what we see in the book of Acts—God confirming His message when believers were faithful to preach it. Now if the evidence of the Kingdom in Jesus' life meant healing, deliverance and salvation, then the evidence of the Kingdom in His followers' lives should be the same. And it is. Today, we're going to look at four different times in Paul's ministry to the Gentiles and see if this pattern holds true.

Continue by explaining that the first instance took place at the island of Cyprus (journey to "Cyprus" and act out the action with the volunteer). Paul and Barnabas have just been prayed over and sent out as missionaries (see Acts 13:2-3). Read Acts 13:4-12 and then explain that Paul arrived on the island of Cyprus and traveled all over it, sharing the Word of God, and eventually came to Paphos—the capital city of Cyprus in that day. By preaching the Word, Paul was directly confronting the powers of darkness that were blinding the minds of the people there and restraining them from receiving Jesus (see 2 Corinthians 4:4). The sorcerer tried to persuade the Roman proconsul against Paul and his message. When Paul saw this, he turned to the sorcerer and, through the power of the Holy Spirit, exposed the evil that was working through this man to stop the gospel. Paul shared the Word and God confirmed it by showing His authority and power over spiritual darkness. The Roman ruler in Cyprus became a believer as a result of this.

Read Acts 14:8-10 (and then journey to "Lystra"). Explain that Paul was again speaking, this time in Lystra. A man who had never walked in his entire life was listening. As he heard what Paul said, faith began to rise in his heart. Paul could see this man was reaching out to God. He spoke directly to him, telling him to stand up—and the man did! He was completely healed. Paul shared the Word and God confirmed it by showing His authority and power to heal.

Read Acts 16:11-15 (and journey to "Philippi"). Explain that we next find Paul in Philippi looking for a place to pray. Instead he ends up near a river talking with a group of women about the Lord. One of the women there was named Lydia. She was a Gentile businesswoman from a different city. As Paul told them about Jesus, God proved His Word was true by opening up Lydia's heart to receive the message. This is probably the most common way God confirms His Word; He gives people the faith to believe His message. Paul shared; God confirmed. And as a result Lydia's whole household—meaning her family and servants—were saved and baptized.

Read Acts 17:1-9 (and journey to "Thessalonica"). Explain that Paul always did the same thing when he arrived at a new city. He would find the local synagogue and go there to the share the message of Jesus. In Thessalonica, we don't see a miracle of deliverance from spiritual darkness or a dramatic physical healing. Instead we see the gospel message confirmed by people's rejection of it. The non-believing Jews rounded up some men to cause a riot and then blamed it on Paul and his fellow believers. As a result, the people and the city officials were really upset. Paul had to sneak out at night and move on to another city, leaving the believers in Thessalonica to weather the storm of persecution. Paul was faithful to share God's Word, and God confirmed it by allowing a rejection and persecution to occur. Jesus said that many would stumble because of His words; many would find them hard to believe. Rejection or persecution can be considered a sign that His truth is pricking the conscience of unbelievers and in their rebellion they act with hate and fear instead of love and surrender.

Conclude by stating that the pattern is the same in all these cases: Believers preach the gospel; God confirms His Word. The way He confirms His Word may be different each time, but we can depend upon Him to prove that His Word is true.

DIG

Option 1: Confirmation Debate. For this option, you need talkative students and listening ears.

Divide students into two groups and explain that today, we're going to have a little debate about whether or not God still confirms His Word in amazing ways, just as He did in the Early Church. Assign each group a point to argue and allow five to seven minutes for students to come up with their arguments to support their assigned views. If groups get stuck, you can make the following suggestions:

- *For the side arguing that God still confirms His Word:* God hasn't changed; miracles happen all the time but we just don't always recognize them; miracles happen but we don't hear about them; we share the gospel and just don't always see the results.

- *For the side arguing that God has stopped confirming His Word:* In the age of technology, we don't need His miracles as much; people have less faith; He's gotten frustrated with our sin and doesn't get as involved anymore, or we share the gospel and nothing really happens.

Conduct a debate allowing each group a certain amount of time for arguments and rebuttals. Help students identify ways that God has proven His Word in their own lives by discussing the following:

- What's the most supernatural thing that has ever happened to you?
- How did it change your life?
- Why do you think people get discouraged about believing that God will confirm His Word? (*Things don't happen the way that people think they should.*)
- What would you say to someone who feels like God's Word isn't for to-day? (*Don't base your faith in what you have experienced or seen; base your faith on what Gnd has said about Himself in His Word.*)
- How has God proved His Word in your own life? (*Salvation, healing, an-swers to prayer, and so forth.*)

Conclude by stating that God wants each of us to be assured that He will keep His Word. He is entirely faithful and we can count on Him to not only use us to speak His message, but to also confirm that message in a way that brings about His will. It might take longer than we hope or expect, but He will do it.

Divide students into small prayer groups and instruct group members to share one area in their lives where they would like to see God confirm His Word. This could be in the healing of a sick family member, in the salvation of a close friend or in the strengthening of their own personal walk with Jesus—any area where they have spread the Word and are believing God will confirm it. Have students pray for each other in these specific areas.

Option 2: The Different Shapes of Confirmation. For this option, you need just the following story. Share the first part of the following case study:

> Kristi had been active in her church as long as she could remember. She knew all the typical Bible stories told in Sunday School, like stories about Noah, Moses, David, Jesus and Paul. But although she could spout out what happened to which Bible character and when it happened, it hadn't really changed her much.
>
> Then she went to summer camp and something happened. All of a sudden, she started seeing how these very same stories related to her own life. She realized that God was not a boring or distant guy in the sky, but Someone who cared about her and wanted a relationship with her. Not only that, but He wanted her to share about Him with others.
>
> The next day, Kristi spent all day at lunch talking with her cousin Nancy. Kristi explained why Jesus had come to the earth and how He had changed her life. Nancy kind of paid attention, but she didn't ask any questions and changed the subject as soon as possible after Kristi was done talking.

Discuss the following:

- Did God confirm His Word to Kristi?
- Did He confirm His Word to Nancy?
- If you were Kristi, how would you have felt?
- How do we know whether or not God confirms His Word?

Now share the second part of the case study:

> Kristi was pretty bummed after her conversation with Nancy, so much so that she decided not to share about her faith with anyone. It hadn't made any difference in Nancy's life, so why should she keep sharing?
>
> What Kristi didn't know is that although Nancy hadn't been super interested that day, the words had sunk in. The next week, when Nancy was feeling bored and alone on summer break, she remembered what Kristi had said and found her parents' Bible. What she read in the Bible

interested her so much that she decided to start going to church with her best friend, Liz.

Discuss the following:

- Did God confirm His Word to Nancy?
- What does this tell you about His timing?
- How does this make you feel about your role in God's plan?

Summarize by stating that we can't always see what God is doing, so our job is just to keep sharing, believing that He will take His truth and change people's lives with it.

APPLY

Option 1: Away from You. For this option, you need your Bible, the song "Away from You" by the O.C. Supertones (available on the album *Unite* or for download), a way to play the song and several adult leaders.

Begin by stating that the first place God wants to confirm His Word is in our own lives. God wants to show *us* how powerful and real His promises are. Have students close their eyes and listen as you play the song, and then explain the song's message: There is no life away from God. (*Note:* If the lyrics are difficult to understand just by listening, read them aloud before the discussion.)

Read 1 John 5:11-12 and remind the students that one way God confirms His Word is by opening our hearts to receive it (remember Lydia?). Give an opportunity for those who have never responded to the gospel to come forward and pray with the adult leaders.

Option 2: Acts Challenge. For this option, you need worship music (live or recorded).

Give the "Acts Challenge" (see the detailed outline in the conclusion of this unit) by asking students to commit to reading the book of Acts over the next two weeks. (This can be accomplished by reading two chapters a day.) As they read, challenge them to keep a record of every time God acted to confirm His Word. (Of course, you'll have to do this too in order to see if they're correct.) The idea is to get students reading for themselves about the awesome power of God. He will strengthen their faith as they read His Word! Consider offering a special prize to those who complete the challenge and turn in their records.

Close with a time of worship, thanking God for being true to His Word.

REFLECT

The following short devotions are for the students to reflect on and answer during the week. You can make a copy of these pages and distribute to your class or download and print from **www.gospellight.com/uncommon/jh_the_new_testament.zip.**

1—HE KEEPS HIS PROMISES

Go to the fourth book of the Bible and find Numbers 23:19-20.

Deena's mom promised to buy her an iPod if she got straight As. All semester, Deena worked hard because she really wanted an iPod. When her report card came in the mail, Deena was *so* nervous! She waited and waited for her mom to get home from work and couldn't believe her eyes when she saw her grades—all As! Deena spent all of the following weekend listening to music on her new iPod.

God promises us a bunch of things throughout the Bible. Sometimes we might wonder if He is going to come through on His Word. Just like Deena got the iPod her mom had promised, we can trust that God will keep His promises to us. Today, tell God that you love Him and that you are grateful for the way He always keeps His Word.

2—CAN-DO GOD

Mark 11:22-24 talks about mountains and jumping, so hurry up and check it out.
Which of these things can you do on your own (check all that apply)?

- ❑   Bait a fishing hook
- ❑   Make a milkshake
- ❑   Climb up on your roof
- ❑   Iron a shirt
- ❑   Write a computer program

We can do a lot of things for ourselves, but there are some things we simply can't do on our own. God is different because He can do anything. Did you know that God can just speak something into creation and it will be there? Remember Genesis 1:3? "And God said, 'Let there be light.'" He *spoke* and it happened. God can and will do anything that He wants to. That alone should make you want to tell people about Him.

Think of three people you can share with about God's power and make yourself a promise to share with them within the next three days. Now pray that God will remind you to do this. Ready, set, *pray!*

3—THE SPIRIT IS UPON YOU

Quick advice for people in jail is found in Isaiah 61:1.

Jenny was walking through the mall and ran into some friends from school. She began to feel nervous, remembering what her youth pastor said the night before about preaching God's Word. She realized as she approached her friends that God wanted her to tell them about coming to a concert at her church that Friday night.

It was hard, but Jenny took a deep breath and asked. To her surprise, several of her friends said it sounded like fun and accepted her invitation!

You are God's preacher. That's right, God created *you* for His plan, and He wants *you* to tell others about Him. The cool thing about God is that He will never have you do anything that you can't handle. Did you know that? God will take care of everything, and all we need to do is speak about what we know of Him.

Ask God to show you where He wants you to speak about Him this week; then *do it!*

4—WAY RICHER THAN YOU THINK

Turn to Ephesians 1:13-14 and find out how rich you are.

What would you rather inherit?

❏ A car	*or*	❏	A million bucks?
❏ A Twix bar	*or*	❏	Reese's Peanut Butter Cups?
❏ A caboodle	*or*	❏	A video game?
❏ A waterbed	*or*	❏	A basketball?

Being a Christian is like having a really big inheritance. We are given all the riches that God promises us. If you knew how people could get free stuff, wouldn't you tell them? It's the same way with God—when we die, we get free salvation and a huge inheritance.

Now knowing this, who are you going to tell about this free gift? Well, what are you waiting for? Do it!

A LINK IN THE CHAIN

THE BIG IDEA

Each generation of Christians is the next link in the chain of spreading the gospel.

SESSION AIMS

In this session you will guide students to (1) understand how vital their part is in communicating God's message to others; (2) realize that the Holy Spirit is with them and in them, giving them power to do God's will; and (3) gratefully acknowledge the sacrifices Christians have made to see that the gospel message is passed on.

THE BIGGEST VERSE

"For what I received I passed on to you as of first importance: that Christ died for our sins according to the Scriptures, that he was buried, that he was raised on the third day according to the Scriptures" (1 Corinthians 15:3-4).

OTHER IMPORTANT VERSES

Matthew 1:1-16; Luke 3:23-38; John 15:13; Acts 24–26; 2 Timothy 4:1-2,7; Hebrews 11:35-40

Note: Additional options and worksheets in $8^1/_2$" x 11" format for this session are available for download at **www.gospellight.com/uncommon/jh_the_new_testament.zip**.

STARTER

Option 1: Timeline 1. For this option, you need a long roll of newsprint or butcher paper, masking tape and felt-tip pens. Tape the paper to the wall at a comfortable height for students to write on. Draw a horizontal line down the middle of the paper from one end to the other. Label the far left end "Creation" and the far right end "Now." Students will be filling in names to create a timeline.

Greet students and announce that this is the last session about the Early Church, and you're going to start off this session by creating a timeline of God's people from Creation until now. Write the name "Adam" at the creation point of the timeline; then have students call out names and, making sure they know where it fits on the timeline, have them come up and write that name on the paper. Any Bible character or well-known Christian is fair game. (You can make this into a contest by seeing who can think of more names, the girls or the guys.) Some Bible names to include are Noah, Abraham, Moses, Joshua, Samson, Ruth, Samuel, David, Isaiah, Nehemiah, Mary, Peter, Paul and John. (*Note:* If students get stuck, have them turn to the genealogies listed in Matthew 1:1-16 and Luke 3:23-38, or the "Hall of Faith" in Hebrews 11. You can also include modern-day Christians, such as Mother Teresa, Billy Graham or your senior pastor.)

After students have exhausted all the names they can think of, conclude: Ever since Creation, God has used people to spread His message to others. Their lives have made a long, linked chain in the ongoing job of spreading the gospel. From Adam to Moses to David to Paul, faithful people have passed God's message to those who would come after them, and the chain remains unbroken. Write "YOU" under the "Now" part of the timeline.

Transition to the next step by explaining that today we're going to look at our part in keeping this chain unbroken. Each of us is an important part of God's plan to reach the world with His love and power. He wants to use us to bring His message to others.

Youth Leader Tip

Relieve the awkwardness of a wrong answer by offering kind words such as "that was a good thought" to remove some of the sting. This can also communicate that the students' value to the group is not based on having the right answers.

Option 2: Finding Your Place. For this option, you need space for students to move around, some upbeat music and candy or other goodies for prizes.

Greet students and divide them into two equal groups. Create two circles of students, one group on the outside facing in and the other on the inside facing out. You should end up with pairs; one person from the outside circle facing one person from the inside circle. Explain that when you start playing the music, each circle is to move to the left (the two circles will move opposite each other). When the music stops, the people on the outside group are to drop on one knee. Each person on the inside circle is to find his or her original partner and sit down on his or her knee. (*Note*: This game causes great confusion and chaos, so watch that more aggressive students don't trample those who are less competitive.) Eliminate the last partners to find their match and then repeat several times until you end up with a winning pair.

Explain that this game shows how hard it can be to find our place. In all the chaos of the moment, it was easy to get turned around. We've talked about a lot of different people from the Early Church and how they spread the gospel. Each of these people played a part in seeing God's message reach someone else. Whether it was highly visible, such as Peter preaching on the Day of Pentecost, or somewhat quiet like Ananias praying for Paul's eyesight to return, every believer was important to what God wanted to do to pass on the gospel message. You fit into God's plan too. He has a place for you that no one else can fill. When you find your place in His plan, you'll feel that same sense of relief that you did during the game. It's not hard to find that place. God is just waiting to guide you into His perfect plan for your life.

Transition to the next step by explaining that as we'll see in today's session, God wants to use us to pass on His message to others.

MESSAGE

Option 1: What Would You Do for a Buck? For this option, you need your Bible and a handful of dollar bills.

Explain that you're going to play a game called "What Would You Do for a Buck?" Here's how to play: You're going to call up one student at a time and ask him or her to do something outrageous. If the student does what you ask, he or she will get a dollar; if not, you'll call on someone else. (Here are some ideas: singing "The Star Spangled Banner"; removing their shoes and getting four people to smell them; making various animal noises; and making a phone call to Mom to confess something that she doesn't know about—yet!).

End the game by pointing out that sometimes we can be motivated to do things we wouldn't normally do because of the rewards offered. Explain that by the time we reach the end of Acts, Christianity has gone from 120 people gathered in an upper room to thousands of believers in many of the major cities of the Roman Empire. These believers were witnesses to what Jesus had done. Some of them had to do some pretty radical things in order to make sure God's story was shared.

Have students take turns reading through Acts 24:1–26:32. Have each one read three or four verses and then pass off to the next person. Because it is a connected story, they should be able to follow along with interest. When the reading is finished, ask students to identify some of the radical things that Paul was willing to do to make sure the gospel was spread. These should include his willingness to share the gospel while in prison, both before Felix and Festus.

Option 2: Paul's Last Stand. For this option, you need several Bibles, several balloons, a large piece of thick cardboard, masking tape, darts, the questions from "Paul's Last Stand" (found on the next page) cut into strips, and a felt-tip pen. (*Note:* Students will be throwing the darts to pop the balloons, so be sure that the cardboard is thick enough to hold a dart. A thick piece of cork works great too, but that can get a little expensive. Oh yeah, and make sure there's nothing breakable near where you mount the cardboard, such as lamps, students' heads—you get the picture.)

Ahead of time, cut the questions from "Paul's Last Stand" into strips, roll them up and insert them into the balloons, one question per balloon. Blow up the balloons and tape them to the cardboard. (*Note:* Use the last two questions in several balloons so that they come up more than once during the activity.)

Distribute Bibles and explain that we are now going to read about the final recorded witness Paul made for Jesus Christ. At this time, Paul is an older man who has given his whole life to see that God's message reaches everyone who'll hear it. Now he would be arrested and brought to trial before Roman officials to make his final case for what he believes.[1]

Have students take turns reading through Acts 24:1–26:32. Have each one read three or four verses and then pass off to the next person. Because it is a connected story, they should be able to follow along with interest. When the reading is finished, discuss the passage by having students pop a balloon one at a time with a dart. They have to respond to whatever question they get.

Sum up by stating that Paul's life is an example of being faithful to spread God's Word, no matter the personal cost. He found his place in God's plan and

Paul's Last Stand

How many times did Paul come to trial before he was sent to Rome?

Who were the three Roman rulers who heard Paul's case?

What was the accusation against Paul?

Could the Jews prove their charges against Paul?

For what reason was Paul really on trial?

Why do you think the Jews accused Paul?

Which one of the Roman officials found Paul guilty?

To whom did Paul appeal?

Was Paul upset about being in prison?

Paul gave his testimony before Agrippa instead of defending himself. What is one situation in which you should talk about the Lord instead of defending yourself?

What is one circumstance you've had that you could have used to share the gospel?

was obedient to the end. Historians believe that Paul was eventually beheaded by the Roman emperor Nero. Let's take a look at other men and women who sacrificed their lives to see that God's Word would continue on.

DIG

Option 1: Modern-Day Martyrs. For this option, you need a YouTube video about a modern Christian martyr (searching "Voice of the Martyrs" will yield several great options) and a way to present the video to the group.

Explain that persecution always strengthens the Church. As hard as it is to swallow the tragedy of martyrdom (dying for something you believe in), the results are clearly a more empowered and holy Church. Persecution of Christians started during the reign of the Roman emperor Nero around A.D. 62. He was so extreme in the way he had Christians killed that some people considered him to be the Antichrist.

But persecution didn't stop there; people have been martyred all the way through current times. In fact, more Christians have suffered persecution, torture and death in the twentieth century than all the previous centuries combined. We can look at the lives of the men and women who have suffered for their commitment to spreading God's Word and be grateful for what they've given to us.

Show the video clip and then discuss the following:

- What gave this person (or people) the ability to give their life for the gospel? (*They knew the truth of God's Word and realized that their earthly life was not the end of the story. There was a home waiting for them in heaven, and though their lives here on earth might end, it was only the beginning of the eternal lives they would experience forever.*)

- The Early Church father Tertullian said, "The blood of the martyrs is the seed of the church." What does this mean? (*Those who spilled their blood for the gospel actually strengthened the work of God. Their sacrifice helped it grow.*)

- How would you respond if you were faced with the decision to deny Jesus and live or not deny Him and die? (*Field responses gingerly, realizing that fear is a powerful emotion. Students who are afraid of the thought of death may not be comfortable with this discussion.*)

- How can we show our gratitude for the sacrifices others have made so we could hear and believe the gospel message? (*Living a Christlike life and purposely sharing His love with others is the best way to pass on the gift we have received.*)

Option 2: More Modern-Day Martyrs. For this option, you need copies of the prisoner list from The Voice of the Martyrs website (www.persecution.com), paper and pens or pencils. (*Note:* Another good resource is *Jesus Freaks* by DC Talk and The Voice of the Martyrs. This book has a wide variety of stories of people who have stood up for Jesus through the centuries.) Check out the directions on The Voice of the Martyrs website for writing to persecuted Christians around the world.

Explain to the group that all over the world—even as we speak—people are being persecuted for spreading the gospel. Distribute the prisoner lists and ask volunteers to read some of the real-life suffering currently happening to Christians. Allow several minutes for discussion of the different situations; then divide students into small groups to pray by name for the suffering Christians on the list (and for all suffering Christians around the globe!).

Distribute paper and pens or pencils and invite each student to select a name on the list and write a letter of encouragement to that person. As you collect the letters to mail, explain that persecution is tragic, but it can also remind us that what we have in Jesus is more important than what we have here on earth. His Word secures a future of blessings and wellbeing for all of us.

APPLY

Option 1: History Maker. For this option, you need the song "History Maker" by Delirious? (available on the album *King of Fools* or for download) and a way to play the song. (*Note:* In addition to playing the song, consider reading the lyrics to make sure students understand the message.)

Begin by stating that as we end this series of lessons, the one thing that you would like the group to walk away with is knowing that God can and will use each of them to take His Word to the world—whether that's through missionary work in foreign lands or standing up for Jesus right here at home. Whatever we do, God wants to fill our lives with His power and allow us the privilege of being a link in the chain of gospel history. We are so important to what God wants to do.

Play the song, instructing students to listen closely to the words. When it's over, have students join hands for prayer and close the session by asking God to bless and anoint each student to be a history maker for Jesus.

Option 2: Timeline 2. For this option, you need a small piece of chain for each student (available at your local home supply store), the timeline from option 1 in the Starter section and felt-tip pens. (If you didn't choose to do that option, you will also need a long roll of newsprint or butcher paper and masking tape. Ahead of time, tape the paper to the wall at a comfortable height for students to write on. Draw a horizontal line down the middle of the paper from one end to the other. Label the far left end "Creation" and the far right end "Now." Students will be filling in names to create a timeline.)

Begin by stating that someone once said that we only have one generation to reach the next generation. Your part in what God has planned is so important. Without you, the link will not be complete.

Give each student a piece of chain. Explain that this chain is to remind them of what we've talked about these past six weeks. Hold up the chain and point out each link. State that each link in the chain represents someone's decision to be a committed follower of Christ and pass on God's message to others. Hold the last link. Explain that the link stops here with them—their generation holds the end. Will they pass on the gospel message to others around them? Will there be a new link added on?

Read 2 Timothy 4:1-2. Continue by stating that while we may never go to a foreign country to share the gospel, that doesn't make our part in God's plan any less significant. God wants to use us where we live to touch lives with His power and love. The message is His, the power is His, but the decision is ours. Will we submit to His Word or choose our own way?

Have the group close their eyes for a time of prayer. Give an opportunity for students to rededicate and/or commit their lives to the call of God to share His Word. As a sign that they are committing to this, have students come forward and sign their names on the end of the timeline they created at the beginning of this session. Explain that this is a signal that they are going to be, by the grace of God, another link in the chain of spreading the gospel message. Keep the timeline on a wall in the meeting room over the next several weeks as a reminder of this decision.

Close in prayer, asking God to bless and strengthen students to do His will, regardless of any obstacles or challenges to their faith.

REFLECT

The following short devotions are for the students to reflect on and answer during the week. You can make a copy of these pages and distribute to your class or download and print from **www.gospellight.com/uncommon/jh_the_new_testament.zip.**

1—YOUR JERUSALEM

Acts 1:8 now! Please!

Kim is very good about telling her friends about Jesus. She invites them to church and even asks them what they think about God. She also supports a child in a poor country with her own money so the child gets food and is able to go to school.

Kim has a problem, though. Her mom isn't a Christian, and it's hard for her to talk to her mom about God. What advice would you give Kim?

Each of the four places listed in Acts 1:8 can be applied to somewhere near you. Name someone in each of these places who doesn't yet know Jesus.

- Jerusalem = your family/your friends/your neighborhood
- Judea = your school/your community
- Samaria = your nation
- Ends of the earth = other countries

Gods wants His message to reach those who are right next to us, as well as those who live across the globe. Pray for the people on your list daily and ask God to work in their lives to open their hearts to Him.

2—JOIN THE HALL OF FAITH

Do you know a guy named David? Read Hebrews 11:32-38.

Write down the names of three people who have done cool things for you and what they did. (This could be a teacher who helped you with a math problem, your parents who always drive you to your friends' houses or your small-group leader at church who is a great listener.)

1. _____
2. _____
3. _____

In Hebrews, you can read about what people have gone through to further the message of Jesus. What would it take for you to be that kind of person, too?

Ask God to make you into that kind of person. Thank Him for all the people who have gone before you who lived this way.

3—IT'S A BIG JOB

Pound your chest like Tarzan and turn to 2 Corinthians 4:15.

Jason is super shy. He's been a Christian for a while but he's afraid to tell people about Jesus. He thinks that other people would be better at it, so why bother? Jason loves God with his whole heart but just doesn't see himself as an evangelist at all.

Have you ever felt like Jason feels? Even if you're shy, God wants you to tell people about Him. After all, you just might be the only one that someone comes in contact with who is willing to tell him or her about Jesus! God wants *you* to be the person who communicates His Word.

How do you feel about knowing that you have this incredible responsibility? Are you feeling overwhelmed? Share your feelings with God and ask Him to bring someone into your life who's "been there, done that" to help you do what God wants you to do!

4—IMITATE THE LEADERS

Go to the book before James and find the 13th chapter and the 7th and 8th verses.

Check the leaders whose names you know:

- ❑   The president of the United States (or the leader of your country)
- ❑   The pope
- ❑   The governor of your state
- ❑   The news anchor on the local evening news
- ❑   The chief of police in your city

There are all kinds of people who lead in this world. Likewise, there are tons of people who have led the great movements of God throughout time. It is our job to know about what those people have done to lead people toward God.

Think of someone you know who might know who some of these leaders of the faith are. Make a commitment today to ask that person to tell you about just one of those people. If you enjoy hearing that story, then maybe they can tell you more.

Oh, and don't forget to "imitate their faith" (Hebrews 13:7)!

THE ACTS CHALLENGE

The book of Acts is every Christian's history. If you're an American, you learn about the Revolutionary War and the Civil Rights movement in your history class at school. (If you're Kenyan, you learn about colonialism and the Mau Mau Uprising.) Learning about your country's history is an important part of figuring out what it means to be a loyal and contributing citizen—and the same is true for Christians! Getting to know the Church's history helps believers know how to live out our faith here and now.

If you're ready to learn your history, take the Acts Challenge, a two-week reading/study plan of the book of Acts. Follow the reading plan below, checking off each day's reading as you go. As you get to know the very first Christians, you may find that following Jesus means more to you than ever before!

Day	Reading	
1	Acts 1	Acts 2
2	Acts 3	Acts 4
3	Acts 5	Acts 6
4	Acts 7	Acts 8

Day	Reading	
5	Acts 9	Acts 10
6	Acts 11	Acts 12
7	Acts 13	Acts 14
8	Acts 15	Acts 16
9	Acts 17	Acts 18
10	Acts 19	Acts 20
11	Acts 21	Acts 22
12	Acts 23	Acts 24
13	Acts 25	Acts 26
14	Acts 27	Acts 28

ENDNOTES

Session 1: Mary and Martha: Wholehearted Devotion
1. There are three main Marys in the New Testament. The first is Mary the mother of Jesus (see Matthew 1:16-25; Luke 1:27-56; John 19:25-27). The second is Mary Magdalene, who wept on Jesus' feet, wiping them with her hair and anointing them with perfume (see Luke 7:36-50; 8:2). She witnessed Jesus' death (see Matthew 27:56; Mark 15:40; John 19:25), attended Him at His burial (see Matthew 27:61; Mark 15:47), and was the first to see Him after His resurrection (see John 20:1-18). The third was Mary of Bethany, the focus of this session, who was the sister of Martha and Lazarus. Whenever Jesus was in their community, she and her siblings would often offer their home to Him.

Session 2: The Generous Widow: Wholehearted Giving
1. The principle of giving 10 percent of one's income as a tithe originated in Genesis 14:20 when Abraham gave a tithe to Melchizedek, the priest, in order to honor God. This guideline continued in the Old Testament (see Numbers 18:26; Deuteronomy 14:22; 1 Samuel 8:15). In the New Testament, Jesus' references to the tithe occur more in the context of criticizing those who thought their own works would earn God's favor (see Luke 11:42; 18:12). Jesus never abolished the tithe, but He placed the focus back on the heart attitude of the giver—just as He did in His comments about the widow's offering.

Session 3: Zack Attack: Wholehearted Surrender
1. Zacchaeus was a Jew and tax collector for the Romans who made his money by charging more in taxes than he was required to collect. He became rich by stealing from his people—something that was condoned by the Roman government. After Zacchaeus repented, he paid back more than the 120 percent the Old Testament required for restitution (see Numbers 5:5-10).

Session 4: The Centurion: A Trusting Faith
1. The story of the centurion in Luke 7 is the first account we read of a Gentile approaching Jesus. As the commander of 100 men, his duties would have included drilling soldiers; inspecting weapons, food and uniforms; and commanding trooops in camp and on the battlefield. He was wealthy and of such good character that even the Jews admired him—even though he was a Gentile and represented the conquering Roman army. In light of the centurion's position and power, it is noteworthy that he recognized Jesus' greater authority and had faith in His power to heal his servant. The Jews had asked Jesus to do a miracle for the centurion because he had built a synagogue for their community, but Jesus was moved to help him because of his great faith—not because of any good he had done or whom he represented.

Session 5: The Four Friends: An Active Faith
1. This is the first time in Mark that we observe Jewish opposition to Jesus. The teachers of the law were shocked that He claimed that the paralytic's sins were forgiven. By claiming this, Jesus was stating that He was equal with God. The teachers' charge of blasphemy was serious and could lead to death—which it ultimately did, when Jesus was again charged before the Sanhedrin (see Mark 14:53-65).
2. The way houses were built in those days, there was often an outside staircase to the roof, and roofs were made of clay supported by mats of branches and wood beams. Given this, the four friends would have had to first carry the man up the stairs, then break through the clay, pull back the branches, and lower the man between the beams. They were very dedicated friends!

Session 6: The Leper: A Desperate Faith
1. Leprosy, a disease mentioned frequently in the Bible, was a slow-progressing disease characterized by scabs and white shining spots on a person's skin. Leprosy was incurable at the time, and because it was highly contagious, it rendered its victims "unclean" and forced them to live

in a separate location outside of the community. Although leprosy can now be cured, it still exists and is found most commonly in Palestine, India, China and Japan.

Unit 1 Conclusion: Get to Know the Four Gospels
1. Adapted from *The Open Bible, Expanded Edition, New King James Version* (Nashville, TN: Thomas Nelson, Inc., 1985).

Session 7: Empowered by the Holy Spirit
1. Luke first presents the concept of being a witness in Acts 1:8. This concept is so dominant in the book that almost everything that follows somehow relates to witnessing. Interestingly, Luke establishes this theme as coming from the very mouth of Jesus Christ, making it clear that it is through the power that we are equipped to witness—from our neighbors to the ends of the earth.
2. Wayne Rice, *More Hot Illustrations for Youth Talks* (Grand Rapids, MI: Zondervan Publishing House, 1995), p. 177.

Session 8: From Denier to Defender
1. In Matthew 10:1, when Jesus first sent Peter and the others out, He gave them the power to heal the sick. The Greek word for power in this verse is *exousia*, which carries with it the meaning of delegated authority. In Acts 1:8, however, the word for power is *dunamis*, which implies strength based on inherent power. In other words, the disciples would receive the inherent power of the Holy Spirit, to be expressed through the authority that Jesus had given to them.

Session 9: Let's Eat
1. The account of Peter going to the house of the Gentile Cornelius is the longest story told by Luke in the book of Acts. In fact, the three stories that take up the most space are Peter and Cornelius (see Acts 10–11), Stephen's speech and death (see Acts 6–7), and Paul's conversion (see Acts 9). All three stories are crucial incidents related to breaking the cultural barriers in order for the gospel to move from the Jews to the Gentiles.

Session 10: From Killer to Crusader
1. One resource is *Reproducible Maps, Charts, Timelines and Illustrations* (Ventura, CA: Gospel Light, 1989).
2. Believers were still considered to be Jews in the days immediately following Jesus' ascension, and they naturally continued keeping the Jewish law and attending their synagogues. Rather than being called "Christians," they were referred to as "those who belonged to the Way" (see Acts 9:2). This was one of the more common terms for first-century believers (see also Acts 19:23; 24:14). The term "Christians" was first used in Acts 11:26 at Antioch, and at the time was a derogatory remark meaning "little Christs."

Session 11: Out of the Frying Pan and into the Fire
1. Paul traveled more than 10,000 miles during the course of his ministry. In the course of his travels, he was stoned and left for dead, beaten, shipwrecked, arrested and jailed. He was also described by one writer of the day as a short, bald man with thick eyebrows, crooked legs and a hooked nose. This physical description underscores the fact that it wasn't Paul's great looks that opened the doors of opportunity for him. Those doors opened through the gift of God's grace and allowed him to meet each challenge with strength.

Session 12: A Link in the Chain
1. The right of legal appeal to Caesar was an important prerequisite of Roman citizenship, resting on some five centuries of legal precedent. By the act of appeal (see Acts 25:11-12), Paul took himself out of the jurisdiction of the Jewish courts and of the local Roman government as well.